"Jessica Sitomer's book reminds me of the old adage: 'Give a man a fish and he'll eat for a day. Teach him to fish and he'll eat for a lifetime.' There is no shortage of books on bookshelves in bookstores offering up the Hollywood hopeful a fish (or in most cases, something fishy). Sitomer provides a strategy on how to create a career so you will work (and eat!) for a lifetime."

—Andrew Kreisberg, Co-Executive Producer *Eli Stone*

"Jessica with *AND...ACTION!* has created a productive and effective way of not only guiding the reader through a method of setting attainable goals but also providing for them an enjoyable process in the journey of self discovery."

—Ana Lucia Cottone, Television Programming Executive

"Thinking outside the box and nurturing relationships is the key to being a successful actor. Jessica Sitomer's *AND...ACTION!* will teach you how to do this. The same career building tools she shares here will also help you balance your life when you get to wear many hats in this field. Run to get this book!"

—Diane Farr, Actress *Numb3rs*
Author *The Girl Code*

"Being a writer/director and working full-time at a production company requires a lot of time management and organization skills. Jessica Sitomer's book, *AND...ACTION!* gives you the tools to juggle the many hats you may wear as you build a successful career in the entertainment industry."

—Sharon Steinhauser, Radar Pictures

"Jessica Sitomer's book *AND...ACTION!* is fantastic! It clearly delineates steps you can take to build your career and realize your goals. It gives you wonderful proactive tools to move your career to the next level. *AND...ACTION!* literally thrusts you into action and, as Jessica puts it, gets you working smart not hard—in other words, effectively. The philosophies, business tools, information, and advice she imparts will inspire you and open up your thinking. She combines the creative with the practical. Among other things, she translates proven, successful tactics from the business world and applies them to the entertainment industry, which is invaluable. I work with Jessica as a career coach and have been excited, motivated, and empowered by the work that we do. This book encapsulates and codifies all of the gems she shares one-on-one. I can't recommend *AND...ACTION!* enough. It will galvanize and propel you, and you will reap the rewards!"

—Juliet Landau, Actress *Ed Wood, Buffy the Vampire Slayer, Angel*
Director of the upcoming *Take Flight: A Gary Oldman Documentary*

"As an actor, I realize the importance of perseverance during the ups and downs of a career in the entertainment industry and how important it is to treat your career as a craft and a business. As an acting coach, I've seen a lot of actors get frustrated when they don't know what more they can do to get jobs. I used to feel powerless because I didn't know how to help my students create opportunities. Jessica Sitomer changed that. Her work with my students helped them book more jobs in the last year than in the entire previous eight years of the studio combined. It has changed the attitude and culture in our acting community. We have gone from a group of artists hoping that our agents, managers, or acting gods would do something for us, to a group of self-empowered business people with a plan. We don't wait for the phone to ring anymore. We build our business. We work at it. We control our destiny.

"AND…ACTION! is a great book for giving you a fresh take on new approaches to the business side of your career. I've recommended Jessica Sitomer to my classes and seen how the students who've taken her workshops have created changes in their careers and their attitude toward the pursuit of work. If you want to make a living from your art, AND…ACTION! will give you the tools you need to persevere through this lifelong marathon!"

—Brad William Henke, Actor *Choke, SherryBaby, October Road, Dexter, World Trade Center, North Country*

"Using the techniques Jessica shares in AND…ACTION!, I have created relationships with people and worked on projects that I had only dreamed of. Even my passive income went to well over six figures. Read this book to make a change or create something new in your life whether that is more work in your category or doing something entirely different!"

—Ed Gutentag, Director of Photography

"Jessica Sitomer's book AND…ACTION! provides outstanding coaching techniques in a unique and enjoyable format. As a coach, I'm guessing you'll see the benefits of reading this book many times over and get something new from it each time, just as I did. What you focus on the first time will be what you need to learn now. Then as you master those techniques, re-read the book and you'll hear different chapters speaking to you ready to be mastered next. Get ready to feel empowered as you read AND…ACTION! and easily understand how you are going to create the career of your dreams."

—Jae M. Sabol, Coach, Licensed Trainer of NLP, and Author of the upcoming *Happiness is the Color You Paint It*

"Jessica's coaching program turbo charged my life. After many years in the entertainment industry, she helped me find a brand new direction. *AND...ACTION!* incorporates the tools that she used to open me up to live a much sweeter, happier life. I will be eternally grateful."

—Jane LaBonte, Publicist for the Oscars and
the Cheetah Conservation Fund in Namibia

"Jessica Sitomer is the definition of pro-active. She responds to life like an artist responds to a blank canvas. She masterfully blends imaginative possibilities with the resources available to manifest outcomes that others only hope will magically occur. Jessica's true gift is her desire and ability to help others to create positive change in their lives."

—Stacey Jill Zackin, MSW & Certified Life Coach

"*AND...ACTION!* is a well-written book that is not just specific to the Entertainment field but can be used by most professionals in the workforce. I especially liked the end-of-chapter And...Action! assignments. I feel from my experience in sales, when I write my goals and objectives down on paper it's more concrete then when I think about them.

"*AND...ACTION!* is straightforward, easy to read, and a fun way of learning. I would recommend it to everyone."

—Wendi Walkes, Sales Representative for Cengage Learning

and...Action!

POWERFUL, PROVEN, AND PROACTIVE STRATEGIES
TO ACHIEVE SUCCESS IN THE ENTERTAINMENT INDUSTRY

JESSICA SITOMER

Library of Congress Control Number: 2008935571

© 2008 Jessica Sitomer.
Cover and Interior designed by Amanda Carver, © 2008 Cold Tree Press
Cover Photograph © iStockphoto.com / pederk
ISBN-13: 978-1-58385-284-2
ISBN-10: 1-58385-284-0

TABLE OF CONTENTS

Where do you want to be in twenty years? Where do you need to be in ten years, five years, and then one year to make that possible?

If you're not getting what you want, what do you need to do differently?

The criteria for setting career goals

Creating a one-year business plan

The Contact List

Re-establishing old relationships

INTRODUCTION

*F*ADE IN:

So, you want to find success in the Entertainment Industry? How do you get the edge over your competition to create the career of your dreams when so many others have failed?

Perhaps you're thinking about a career in entertainment and getting confused while researching what it takes. Maybe you're studying your craft and struggling because you don't know how to get work. You may have been in the industry for years and are frustrated by not getting your desired results. Possibly you want to go in a new direction but you're lost not knowing where to start. Whatever stage you're at in your career, this book is for you!

Most people don't succeed in the entertainment business because they believe that if they are good at what they do, their talents will be discovered. In an ideal world, this would be true. In the real world of the entertainment business, the stress is on *business*—it comes first. Like it or not, this makes *you* a freelance business owner. Unlike most business owners, you probably haven't gone to business school. Don't let that intimidate you; keep pursuing your dream! Consider *And...Action!* your business school for the entertainment industry.

You may be one of those people who, having read career books, feel that you have acquired business tools. Yet, you are still discouraged by your lack of success. Career books generally only deal with career strategies. This can be ineffective if there are other issues in your life that present obstacles. My book is special because I present career strategies within the context of lifestyle issues. What you do in all aspects of your life affects your career as much as your career affects your life. Therefore, the focus is on the whole picture. By digging deeper, you can discover what is preventing you from enjoying the success you desire.

Has this desired success eluded you because you don't know how to generate work? As a career coach in the entertainment industry for the last fifteen years, when I ask clients what they do to generate work, I hear responses like this: "I have a list of people, and once a week (or month or year) I call them all to see what they're up to and to tell them that I'm available for work." Many people do the same things over and over to get work yet expect different results. Not to worry; I will give you new ideas to get you thinking outside the box in exciting and productive ways you've never imagined. You will begin seeing results within the first five months if you commit to these exercises.

Another problem my clients face is the general sense of being overwhelmed. Is this a stumbling block for you too? Specifically, you as many others, may be experiencing fears, rejection, disappointment, and confusion. You may even find yourself questioning how long you can go on in your career quest. To compound the enormity of these issues is the feeling that you have to confront them by yourself. Do you feel as if you have to do it all on your own? Do you sit in front of your computer alone? Well, you're not alone in your experience! Every person I have coached has felt that way.

Now, you have an instructive "companion" to guide you along your journey: *And…Action!* While the format is absolutely single-user friendly, you might consider gathering some friends or colleagues to work through the book as a group. I suggest that you read it once for an overview, then read one chapter a week, in sequence. Answer the chapter questions in a journal, and do the assignments. For some additional motivation, you can rent the chapter's movie. The lessons are designed to make the process creative, effective, and fun.

My personal journey began in the 1990s. I trained as an actress for five years, both in New York and Los Angeles. Just before graduation I landed my first independent feature through someone who knew me in school; I didn't even have to audition. I thought, great, this is easy! But when I got back from location from my wonderful experience in Oregon, I wondered, now what? How do I get work? I had no idea. Therefore, I sought out advice. I also learned a lot by trial and error. Over the past fifteen years I've succeeded in producing two television pilots, writing numerous feature scripts and television specs, acting in various projects, directing short films, working in development for Debra Hill

Productions, and simultaneously creating a position for myself as the career coach for the Cinematographers Guild. In that position, I coached more than one thousand people one-on-one, ran group sessions, led seminars, and created a mentor program. As a result of this and simultaneously working in the industry, I have discovered the tools, strategies, and mindsets that I address in this book. You get in fifty-two chapters what took me my whole career to learn!

It's already been established that the entertainment industry is a business. I have coupled that fact with the adage, "Nothing succeeds like success." It made sense, therefore, to look to the business world for tools that have proven track records of being successful. Having done this, I then adapted these techniques to specifically apply to our industry. However, considering the philosophy behind *And...Action!*, its audience is not limited to the entertainment world. The techniques are useful to those who run their own businesses or who work in sales. Whether you're a real estate agent or a personal trainer, if you want to build your business (and if you love movies), this program is for you, too!

With *And...Action!*, the potential to grow your contacts, to get jobs, and to find fulfillment doing what you love is limitless. Once you master the tools and mindsets, you will be in a position to reap the benefits this industry offers: artistry, great projects, choosing the people with whom you want to work, and lots of money.

If you knew there were steps that you could *actively* take that would, in *only* one year's time, give you the edge over your competition and radically improve your productivity in helping you to achieve your career goals would you say, "That's too long"? Would you say, "That's too much of a commitment"? I don't think so. Since you're serious about your profession, I believe you would welcome the challenge. You've waited long enough to make your dreams come true. Let each week unfold new adventures and insights to a truly fulfilling career and life!

ACKNOWLEDGMENTS

I would like to thank my parents Stephen and Elaine Sitomer, my sister, Julie, and my fiancé, Sean Waxman. They are my constant sources of encouragement, support, and inspiration as I continue on my amazing journey.

To Heidi Wall and Suzanne Lyons, thank you for giving me my first "tool belt" and the confidence to navigate this business of entertainment.

I am fortunate and grateful to have had wonderful teachers and mentors: Diane Farr who is always my go-to girl; Andrew Kreisberg, writer extraordinaire; Julia Buchwald who mentored me early on from an agent's point of view; Elaine Goldsmith-Thomas who inspired me to move to LA and taught me many valuable lessons; Mark Pellington who mentored me on directing; Lolita Davidovich, my first actress mentor; Lew Wells who taught me all about physical production while producing my first short film; George Spiro Dibie, aka "Sexy," who continues to help me in any way he can; Lucia Cottone, my teacher in the business and in life; Brad William Henke, the most inspirational acting coach out there and a great example of a dedicated and talented actor;

Jason Ensler who lets me hang around his sets and learn; Rick Sessinghaus, a great coach, speaker, and golfer; and Patrick List, aka "P-Listy," my development guru who reads every draft of every script I write. Thanks to you all.

To the many courageous members of Local 600 who allowed me to guide you and to contribute to your success; I honor you and your commitments to your dreams. To Bruce, Steve, Tim, and the Executive Board, thank you for believing in me and encouraging me to make a difference at your guild. Ellen McCrea gets special thanks for being my greatest advocate and sounding board!

To the many others I've coached through the years, thank you for all you've taught me. I wish you continued success!

As for my friends Jenny Bara, Chelsea, Brian and Lisa, Fry, Jamie C., the Sharkeys, Wen & Mich, Sharon, Stacey, Marty, and Andrea, thanks for always being there.

A very special thank-you to Iris Waxman. She advised me during every step of the writing of this book. And thank you to Rachel and Amanda at Cold Tree Press whose expertise has made publishing my first book an amazing experience!

AUTHOR'S NOTE

This book is a career coaching tool regarding the use of business, sales, marketing, and personal development techniques for people in the entertainment industry. To illustrate the points I am making, I use tie-ins to significant movies.

Each chapter title is based on a motion picture and is used here for educational purposes pursuant to the Fair Use Doctrine.

My book is not endorsed by or affiliated with any of the performers, directors, producers, or screenwriters who created these movies or by the studios that produced and distributed them, and the titles are used here for purposes of teaching only.

Readers who are interested in seeing these wonderful movies in their entirety are encouraged to buy or to rent copies of the movies from authorized sources.

and...Action!

BACK TO THE FUTURE week 01

Marty McFly is fortunate enough to know Doc Brown, a scientist who has created a time machine. Thanks to time travel, and two sequels, Marty is able to visit the past and the future.

Isn't it amazing how motivating it is to get a glimpse of your future and not like it? In this first week, to help you start a successful beginning or re-write of your career, let's go "back to the future" and take a glimpse. I say back because I'm guessing you've thought about your future before. If you haven't, then you'll be starting with a clean slate. What's in store for your future? If you continue pursuing work in the same way you are now, getting the same results, will you realistically be where you want to be in twenty years? Are you setting yourself up to get what you want? If not, like Marty, go "back to the future" to see what it has to offer. You can return to the present and make some positive changes!

Start by visiting the future of your dreams. Decide what you want your career path to be and envision it. It's extremely important to take the time to think this through. Find a place where it's quiet and you can get comfortable: a cozy chair, under a tree, in a bubble bath. Ask yourself, where do you want to be in twenty years? Imagine your career goals and desired success have come to fruition. On what kind of projects are you working? In what capacity are you working? With whom are you working? How much money are you making? Imagine a specific moment twenty years into your future when you're having the ideal day on a job. What is this moment? Where are you? Who's around you? What do you see, hear, smell, feel, and taste? Really allow your imagination to take you away.

Once you've given a lot of thought to the future that you would like to create for yourself, start coming back to the present. As you do, stop at ten years from now and ask yourself, "Where would I need to be to realize my twenty-year vision?" Next, come back to five years from now and ask yourself the same question. Come back to one year from now and ask it, again. Envisioning your future is a great way to start!

1. Do the visualization exercise. Imagine it is twenty years from now. On what kind of projects are you working? In what capacity are you working? With whom are you working? How much money are you making? Imagine a specific moment twenty years into your future when you're having the ideal day on a job. What

is this moment? Where are you? Who's around you? What do you see, hear, smell, feel, and taste?

2. Write what you have visualized.

_____

_____

_____

_____

_____

_____

_____

_____

_____

_____

_____

_____

_____

_____

_____

_____

_____

02

50 FIRST DATES

enry Roth thinks he has finally found the girl of his dreams only to discover that she has short-term memory loss and forgets about him the next morning. Henry quickly observes that when he repeatedly tries the same tactic, it doesn't work. He tries new ones: tying himself up, letting his wacky friend attack him, and putting a penguin in harm's way. Being so committed to making it work with Lucy, he turns to the experts: Lucy's dad and brother. By talking to them he begins finding ways to make his quest more successful until finally he achieves his dreams.

If you're not getting what you want in your career, what do you need to do differently? It can be hard to figure out if you're doing everything you think there is to do. The good news is there's always more you can be doing; you only need to find out what that "more" is. Know that you're not alone. When I ask people what they are doing to generate work for themselves, I tend to hear particular answers over and over again. Many say that they're reading the trades/breakdowns and submitting their resumes/reels/pictures. Others report calling all of the people they know to inform them of their availability for work. Another popular response is that they have agents submitting them.

There are about two more answers that are job classification specific. But overall, people who are not business savvy are doing the same five things. Moreover, since repeatedly doing these things doesn't meet with success, people feel frustrated, bitter, and angry. It's time to try something else!

I offer an analogy to illustrate my point. Let's say you are accustomed to going through the same door to enter your market. One day you arrive and the door has been turned into a wall with sheetrock and a new coat of paint. It wouldn't make sense to stand there pounding on the wall trying to get in; you must look for a new door!

Doing the same things over and over again and expecting different results is the definition of insanity. But it can be pretty frustrating if you don't know how or where to look for other ways of doing things. This book is going to give you ideas and tools for trying new ways to generate work. It will also show you how to take the work you're already doing to a deeper level so you will see better results. There are so many possibilities that can come from the new techniques you'll be learning, so be open to them and your career will change!

and...*Action!*

1. Write everything you do to generate work for your career.

_____

_____

_____

_____

2. Is there anything you don't do because you've been avoiding it?

_____

_____

_____

_____

3. Write any ideas/possibilities that you can think of to generate work and new working relationships, whether you would do them or not.

_____

_____

_____

_____

4. Are there things you've thought of doing but decided not to because you were unsure how they would be perceived?

_____

_____

_____

_____

5. If you already know an industry expert (someone who is successful in the industry) ask him or her to look at your list and give you one new action that you can take to further your career.

Industry expert: _____

Advised action: _____

_____

_____

_____

Mark your calendar to re-read your answers in this section every twelve weeks. You may or may not find that your opinion has changed on taking action.

week 03

SAY ANYTHING...

When asked by his girlfriend's father what he wants to do with his life, Lloyd Dobler replies, "I don't want to sell anything, buy anything, or process anything as a career. I don't want to sell anything bought or processed, or buy anything sold or processed, or process anything sold, bought, or processed, or repair anything sold, bought, or processed. You know, as a career, I don't want to do that."

While his response made for an entertaining scene, it did nothing in the way of helping his career advance because his goal was unclear. Your goal should be a specific, measurable, breakthrough result that answers yes to the following questions:

Is it a stretch—is it more than you've pushed yourself to do in the past?

Is it doable?

Does it have a single focus?

Is it measurable?

Is it easy to understand—can you say it in ten seconds, twenty-five words or less?

Does it make you nervous and also excited?

To choose a goal, figure out what is missing in your career. Do you need more work, better work, or different work? Do you know enough people who can hire you, or do you need more relationships? Do you know a lot of people but not well enough to be hired by them? Do you need to improve your skills or to work on your craft? What is the next step for you? As an example, suppose you decide you want more work. You realize the reason you haven't been working is because you don't know enough people who can hire you. Once you are clear about what you need, choose measurable results for your goal so you know when you've achieved it. An example of this would be, I will create three new relationships with people who can hire me as a _____ this week. Is that measurable? Yes. Is it possible to do? If so, is it a stretch for you to create three in a week's time? Is it easy to understand and does it have a single focus? Yes. Does it excite you to meet new people knowing they can hire you? Does it make you a little nervous? If yes, you've met all the criteria for creating a successful goal.

Imagine yourself at the point of completion, the point where you'll know you've accomplished your goal, and imagine how it feels. If your goal is to meet three new people, imagine you're sitting at a coffee shop, shaking hands with a man as he gets up to go and hearing him say, "It was great to meet you. I'll call you when I have a job for you." You thank him, sit down after he leaves, and open your goal book to write the number three in red.

When visualizing yourself at the point of completion, you want your imagination to get very detailed, allowing you to feel the feelings of accomplishing your goal. See what and who are around you, hear the sounds and conversations, and taste the flavors of whatever you imagine is being served. Feel the feelings of the paycheck in your hand. Experience the reaction of seeing your increased bank statement.

Follow this success formula: make a plan to achieve your goal, put that plan into action, evaluate whether your actions are working, take different actions until your goal has been achieved.

Be aware that as you pursue your career goals, circumstances will change, your plans may change, and life may throw you distractions. Hold onto that picture of your end result, that feeling of greatness when you know you've achieved your goal.

Design a goal for the week.

By _____, I will have or be:
      (one week from today)

_____

_____

_____

_____

_____

week 04
MRS. DOUBTFIRE

aniel Hillard is not the most responsible guy, which leads to his wife divorcing him and the loss of custody of his children. Realizing the error of his ways, he creates a plan to disguise himself as Mrs. Doubtfire, a wonderful housekeeper and nanny. It is through the execution of his plan that he creates a successful new life with his family.

If you want to succeed, you need a plan. In the first week, you visualized where you want to be in twenty years, and then you imagined where you needed to be in ten years, five years, and one year from now. What did you come up with when you visualized where you need to be one year from now?

On _____ _____, _____ I will be/have:
                 (month)   (day)   (year)

_____

_____

_____

_____

_____

Many people in the freelance industry don't use one of the most important tools in business: *a business plan*. Creating a business plan is simple. You start by looking at where you want to be in one year, determining what smaller goals must be accomplished, and breaking those smaller goals down over the next twelve months. There are many possibilities for career successes over the next twelve months that will get you one year closer to your twenty-year dream. Let's use as an example an actor whose twenty-year visualization has him backstage after winning the Academy Award. He's on the phone with his agent who's telling him that he can have his pick of roles and his price tag is now the highest in Hollywood.

To be back stage at the Oscars in twenty years, our actor, who currently has very few union credits on his resume, decides that in one year he must have three more co-star credits, get an agent, and meet fifty people who can help him get hired (producers, directors, writers, and casting directors).

Breaking those goals down over twelve months, he chooses to meet five new people per month for the first ten months. He gives himself until month six to get his agent. He spreads out his three jobs over the final quarter of the year, knowing that he'll have nine months to do the work it takes to get those jobs using the techniques he'll be learning each week in this book.

There are different ways for you to categorize career successes. Some examples are number of days worked, amount of money earned, new people met, networking events attended, studio or sets visited, and number of jobs obtained.

Write five career successes that you would like to accomplish by one year from today. You can break them down over a twelve-month period by using numbers to make it specific.

1. _____

_____

2. _____

_____

3. _____

_____

4. _____

_____

5. _____

_____

In the timetable on the next page, fill in the months at the top and your goals down the left side. Add in personal goals, as well, to maintain balance. Then mark under the specific months when you want to accomplish your goals.

If a goal is something you plan to achieve once, you will write the number 1 in the month you plan to accomplish it. If you plan to achieve a goal multiple times, for example booking a co-star role or meeting new people, you can break each goal down over a twelve-month period by using numbers to make it specific. If you want three co-star roles in one year choose the months you want to book each one and write the number 1 in them. If you want to meet sixty people in a year, choose how many people you want to meet each month and number accordingly, leaving months open at the end of the year to make up for any months you didn't achieve your goal.

SAMPLE YEAR TIMETABLE (ACTOR)

GOAL	J	F	M	A	M	J	J	A	S	O	N	D
1. *get agent*						1						
2. *book co-star role*									1	1	1	
3. *meet new people*	5	5	5	5	5	5	5	5	5			
4. *take vacation*				1								1

YEAR TIMETABLE

GOAL													
1.													
2.													
3.													
4.													
5.													
6.													
7.													
8.													
9.													
10.													

Knowing what goals you want to accomplish during the next year is the first step to creating your business plan. Now that you know what you want to do, the following chapters will teach you how to achieve your goals.

FLATLINERS

M edical students exploring near-death experiences makes for a good movie, but what I want to turn your attention to is one of *Flatliners*'s stars: Kevin Bacon. You may have heard of the Hollywood game called "Six Degrees of Kevin Bacon." Kevin has acted in so many projects with such great talents (in *Flatliners* alone he worked with Julia Roberts, Kiefer Sutherland, William Baldwin, Oliver Platt, and Hope Davis) that actors look at whom they've worked with and figure out in how many degrees they are connected to Kevin Bacon. I worked on a pilot called *Wild Oats* starring Paul Rudd who starred in a movie with Jennifer Aniston who starred in a movie with Kevin Bacon. See how it works? While it's a fun game for actors, it's a reality for anyone who wants to make it in the entertainment industry—it's "who you're connected to."

In order to accomplish your one-year plan, you must have a realistic look at whom you have relationships with in the industry, how strong those relationships are, and how many you have.

When I coach someone for the first time, I have him create what I call a Contact List. A Contact List is a list of everyone you know in the industry broken down by classification and rated by how well you know each person. There are many uses for this list. First, just the action of putting it together can remind you of people with whom you've been out of touch. Second, it gives you a perspective. If you've been out of work and you have only ten names on your list, you don't know enough people to hire you. If you know two hundred people but rate them low, you're missing deep relationships. You now know that an action you need to take is to build those relationships. If you know two hundred people with high ratings and you're not working, it's most likely because you're not asking for help or your attitude is an obstacle.

Here is a sample of what a Contact List looks like:

SAMPLE CONTACT LIST

(5) strong relationship/friendship
(1) worked/met once or twice
You decide what 4, 3, and 2 mean on your rating scale.

[Note: All names are fictional]

PRODUCERS

(3) Stacey Share

(2) Brian Blazer

(1) Jerry Bruckenheimen

DIRECTORS

(5) Steven Bergspiel

(5) Ron Poward

(4) Judd Bigtoe

(3) Cameron Hawk

(1) Penny General

ACTORS

(1) Julia Roperts

(4) Tom Ranks

(5) Reece Forkspoon

(2) Keifer Northerland

(5) Brad Manke

WRITERS

(2) Cameron Caw

(3) Nora Peppron

(4) Richard Hugh

DIRECTORS OF PHOTOGRAPHY

(5) Vilmos Manzsig

(3) Stephen Postcard

(4) Mike O'Stay

(1) Sandi Bissel

(5) George Gyro Dobie

EDITORS

(4) Brent Gray

(2) Smith Leigh

PRODUCTION DESIGNERS

(5) Nate Crawling

(5) Jefferson Parsley

(2) Naomi Han Sho

MANAGERS

(5) Brian Cooper

AGENTS

(3) Julia Waldbuch

MISCELLANEOUS

(3) Laney Goldtom—Studio head

(5) Julie Gayle—craft service

(3) John Stone—gaffer

(4) Paula Market—gaffer

(5) Jay Rey—PA

(1) Andy McLaughlin— development

(3) Garrett Winder— Ass't to Tom Cluise

(2) Jeff Watson—grip

(5) Ralph Rand— Julia Ropert's pool man

(4) Delia May—script supervisor

The list is also useful in getting to the people you want to know. When I hear people say, "It's all who you know," it always sounds like a complaint, as if it's an obstacle. I suppose it could appear to be so if you don't feel you know the right people.

Here are some ideas for creating a Contact List:

+ Design it on a computer in Word, Excel, or another database program
+ Make it on a corkboard using pushpins and colored paper
+ Draw it on poster board using colored markers

Because there are truly "six degrees of Kevin Bacon" in this industry, it is possible to get to know whomever you want. In next week's chapter, you'll choose whom you want to know. Refer to the people on your Contact List to see if they have a direct introduction connection. If not, they may know someone who may know the people you want to meet (utilize the degrees of separation).

1. Make your Contact List. You can use the sample in this chapter. Or be more creative in your format—as long as you are able to keep adding to it and changing the rating numbers as you deepen your relationships with people.

2. In your journal, answer the follow questions to evaluate your Contact List:

+ In what classifications do you need more relationships?
+ With whom do you want to deepen your relationships?
+ With whom have you been out of contact? Do you want to get back into contact with them?

week 06
THE BIG CHILL

When a funeral reunites a group of old college friends, they use the occasion as an opportunity to get reacquainted. They discuss old idealisms, dreams come true, unattained goals, and in the end, they are happy to have been reunited.

In Week 5, I had you evaluate your Contact List. Before I have you focus on meeting new people, I'd like to address the people you've lost contact with and those with whom you would like to deepen your relationship.

Getting back in touch with people is easier than you think if you have current contact information for them. The biggest obstacle in doing this is the one you create. It's the conversation you have with yourself about how it looks when you've been out of touch for so long or why you're getting back in touch now. It's these, and all of the other concerns you imagine, that stop you from making the call.

Ask yourself these questions:

1. Why do you want to get back in touch with this person?

_____

_____

_____

2. What were the traits of this person that you really liked?

_____

_____

_____

3. What are your concerns about contacting this person now?

_____

_____

_____

4. If none of your concerns came to be and you had a great conversation with this person, what are the possibilities that could come from getting back in touch with her?

_____

_____

_____

When you want to make a call that makes you uncomfortable, you have to be sure that the motivation of the desired outcome outweighs the fear of making the call. In other words, the great opportunities that you imagine could happen if you get back in touch have to outweigh the fear of your concerns. When you're about to pick up the phone and the voices in your head start reminding you that it's been too long, he won't remember you, he's going to think that you want to use him, change your focus to all of the exciting possibilities that you imagined could come from this call.

What I had you do in questions three and four was to write your thoughts on the call if it were to go badly or if it were to go well. In fact, the call could go either way. But you have no way of predicting the outcome, nor do you have control over how the person you're calling will react. The one thing you do have control over is on which thoughts you're going to focus. Since they are both made up by you, why not choose to focus on the possibility thoughts because they will empower you to make the call. The only sure thing is—if you don't make the call, you will get no reaction from the person. Should your concerns come to fruition or if your call goes unreturned, you didn't lose anything because you were out of touch anyway. But if the person is glad you called and happy to hear from you, it was well worth pushing through your fears!

One way to renew a relationship or contact is through a personal note. Holidays, birthdays, and anniversaries are great times to get back on someone's radar. But if there is no occasion at the time you choose to reconnect, a simple note will do. The following is a sample note for re-establishing a relationship:

> *Dear "Old Friend,"*
>
> *I hope this note finds you well. It has been a long time since we worked together on The Dog Ate My Homework. I was going through an old address book when I came across your name and thought it would be good to get back in touch with you. It's been wonderful watching how your career has blossomed through the years, and I've made a point to see every picture you've done in the movie theaters.*
>
> *I have been busy working as a _____ and have enjoyed working on such projects as Tim's Gateway and The Football Diaries. It would be great to catch up over a cup of coffee. You can reach me at 555-1212, or I'll follow up with you in a week to see if we can set something up.*

If you don't know how to reach this person a few ideas are to contact his guild, search the Internet (Google, IMDb, or the Hollywood Creative Directory), or call any mutual acquaintances.

On your Contact List you may have discovered people with whom you are in touch, but with whom you'd like to deepen the relationship.

Answer these questions:

1. Why do you want to deepen your relationship with this person?

_____

_____

_____

2. What are your common interests?

_____

_____

_____

3. How can you incorporate your common interests into a fun reason to get together? If you both like fly fishing for example, perhaps you can organize a fishing trip. If the person works on a show that you like, perhaps you can request a visit to the set.

_____

_____

_____

In many cases, it's just a matter of picking up the phone and asking, "How are you doing?" Do keep in mind that someone working on a project may not have the time to catch up. Therefore, at the onset of the call ask if this is a convenient time for your conversation. If the answer is no, ask when it would be a good time to inquire about...

Another good strategy is to have a second reason for calling in your back pocket, something that only that person can answer.

1. Re-establish three relationships.

2. Call one person with whom you would like to deepen your relationship. Make a plan to see him, or ask a question that would lead to a follow-up call.

week 07
MR. & MRS. SMITH

r. & Mrs. Smith are a married couple and, unbeknownst to each other, hired assassins. They work for different companies traveling the world with a list of targets to "eliminate," but their secret careers collide when they find out that their next targets are each other.

This week I'm going to have you create a Target List of your own. The difference between your targets and Mr. & Mrs. Smiths' is that they killed theirs—you just want to meet yours.

A Target List is simply a list of the people you want to know. For now, concentrate on the *who*. How you will get to them will come later in the book. Be open to possibilities and put names on your list that are a mix of people who seem to be accessible as well as those who are not.

Whom do you need to know? If you're an actor, you may think casting directors. If you're a director or a writer, you may think producers. If you're a head of a department like a director of photography, you may think directors. The answer may seem simple and obvious. Well, it's not that simple and not always obvious. The answer to the question "whom do you need to know" for whatever classification you are in is everyone! Yes, you start by figuring out who the person who can hire you is, but then you must think outside of the box. If you are hired by directors, who else knows directors? The answer is every head of a department such as editors, production designers, and costume designers because they all get hired by directors, too. Remember that whomever you meet in this business could be a link to a person you want to know.

There are many ways to come up with the names you choose to put on your Target List:

- Look back at your Contact List to see the classifications of people who are missing, then do the research to find out which people in that classification you would like to meet.
- Research existing projects or projects that you've seen to create a list of people you would like to work with in the future.
- Who are the "next-step" people? In other words, who are the people just a step ahead of you and therefore more accessible?

These people may seem out of reach now, but if you take the time to create relationships with them, down the road you could find yourselves working together.

and...*Action!*

1. Make a Target List of the people with whom you would like to meet/work.

1. _____
2. _____
3. _____
4. _____
5. _____
6. _____
7. _____
8. _____
9. _____
10. _____
11. _____
12. _____
13. _____
14. _____
15. _____
16. _____
17. _____

18. _____
19. _____
20. _____
21. _____
22. _____
23. _____
24. _____
25. _____

Another type of Target List is a list of projects on which you would like to work. Once you come up with this list you can research the people who work on them. Sometimes it's easier for your contacts to recognize names of projects and then to think of people they know who are working on them.

2. Make a Target List of projects on which you would like to work.

1. _____
2. _____
3. _____
4. _____
5. _____
6. _____
7. _____

8. _____

9. _____

10. _____

11. _____

12. _____

13. _____

14. _____

15. _____

16. _____

17. _____

18. _____

19. _____

20. _____

21. _____

22. _____

23. _____

24. _____

25. _____

week *08*

BACK TO SCHOOL

hornton Melon, a hugely successful businessman, enrolls in his son's college and goes "back to school." This businessman shows his skills at creating relationships by throwing the biggest parties, making people laugh, and being bold. While his antics embarrass his son, Jason, it becomes obvious why he is so successful in business.

Knowing people in the industry is essential. You've created a list of the people you want to get to know. We're ready for this week's focus on what it takes to create new relationships.

The mistake most people make when meeting someone for the first time is asking for work. It's important for you to understand that successful people in our industry have many responsibilities. If they are working on a union production there is a lot of money at stake, as well as peoples' jobs and reputations. Therefore, they don't want to take the risk of hiring someone they don't know. Moreover, they don't have to take the risk. Being successful, they've been working for a while and have established many long-standing relationships. On their lists of these people filed in their mental rolodex, there are those who have mortgages to pay, health insurance hours to earn, and kids to put through private school. In other words, people they care about.

Rule #1 for creating relationships:

At first meeting, resist asking for work.

Instead, ask for something they can say *yes* to.

If you were in their position, would you say yes to a stranger you just met? These people haven't any idea how you're going to be on set. You know that you're professional, reliable, and skilled—but they don't. To break into their mental rolodex you must get them to care about you.

How do you get them to care about you? You may have had this experience: you've met someone once, had a two-hour conversation, and gleaned career-changing advice. Yet when you called that person back several months later to say thanks, she had no idea who you are. How, you wonder, can someone have such a great impact on your life and you're not even a blip on the radar? I can tell you that it's not personal. Rather, it's because you thought you had established a relationship with that single conversation, when in actuality, you had not.

Rule #2 for creating relationships:

It takes three conversations to create a relationship.

How do you begin this process? You're meeting new people at a party, screening, set visit, through a friend, or any of the ways you meet new people. What to do? You can ask for advice: business advice and guidance. Have him give you at least one action that you can take to get you to the next step in your career. Ask him what he does to generate work. If he is much farther along than you, ask him to recall when he was in your position and if he knew then what he knows now, what he would do differently. Then get his contact information so you can follow up to tell him how his advice worked for you. Remember, if you find someone gracious enough to advise you for two hours, there is a really good chance that he is giving his time to many people. Therefore, you must do your job and follow up while you're still clearly in his mind, otherwise he will probably forget who you are.

I recommend calling in a month's time so you can act on the advice given and have something to report.

In the first conversation, if you don't want to elicit advice, then ask the person you've met about himself. A great question is, "When did you know that you wanted to do what you're doing?" Everyone in the business has a story in reply to this inquiry. As you get more personal in the conversation, find something that would make a good follow-up. You don't blatantly have to ask for a second conversation, but you should have an idea as to when and what you will be following up about. Remember to get that contact information for that second conversation and call within the month.

If you were to work with people on set you could prove to them that you show up on time, listen, take direction, follow through, pay attention to detail, etc. You can prove all these traits without working with someone simply by following up with a second conversation.

If in a first conversation you are told to: A) join a networking organization, B) read a specific book, and C) make a list of shows you want to work on and ask your friends if they know anyone working on them, take the month to do A, B, and C.

Follow up in conversation two to tell him about your results. He will learn that you're reliable, you listen, take direction, follow through, pay attention to detail, etc. In this second conversation you tell him what worked and what needs more clarification. You ask what he suggests you do for the next month. He is excited about your initiative and inclined to give you more to do. You're creating a win/win situation because you're getting valuable advice, and he feels good because he's giving back to someone who is eager to learn.

Once again, you take the second conversation's advice and call to request the third conversation to discuss your results. If the second conversation was over the phone, you may decide to ask that the third be in person for coffee or lunch, on set, or in your contact's office. Together you discuss the results. By this time, he may be really impressed after seeing how hard you're willing to work. He may care enough about you to give you a break, and if not, he will certainly know who you are when you call with a request down the line.

Suppose you have fifteen people who are advising you and one of them decides to give you your break. You then call the other fourteen people to tell them about the person who gave you the break. Suddenly, a domino effect happens because if that one person hired you, it gives the others the confidence to hire you as well.

Finally, be prepared, especially when asking for advice. The quality of the questions you ask will illustrate where you are in your career. If you're asking questions that you really want to know the answers to, you'll always be genuine and people will want to help you.

Craft five questions to which you really want to know the answers.

1. _____

_____

2. _____

_____

3. _____

_____

4. _____

_____

5. _____

_____

THE SILENCE OF THE LAMBS

I n order to gain a better insight into the warped mind of a serial killer, FBI trainee Clarice Starling talks to psycho-pathic cannibal Hannibal Lecter who used to be a respected psychiatrist. The FBI feels confident that if Clarice interviews the demented prisoner, Lecter may provide psychological clues to the killer's actions.

Nine weeks into this book, you have a clear idea of what you want, whom you know, and whom you want to know. At this point, I'd like to introduce you to the idea of obtaining mentors.

When Clarice needed help, she went to an expert. Whom must you study? A mentor is someone who can give you business advice and guidance. There are different levels of mentors ranging from A-List experts to people who are a step or more ahead of you in your career. I believe you should have as many as you can handle.

As we discussed in Week 8, it takes three conversations to establish a relationship, so plan to have at least three conversa-tions with each mentor. In this chapter, we are going to discuss whom to seek out as mentors. In Week 12, we will discuss how to contact them.

How do you choose mentors? There are many ways. You can start like Clarice and research the experts in your field. Whose career path would you like to emulate? Who is someone you would like to work with in the future?

Look for someone in another classification hiring people in your classification. For example, directors hire all heads of departments and usually have a say in the actors who are hired. If you are an actor or a head of a department, a director can teach you a lot about what you can do to further your career.

Approach someone a step or two ahead of you. A person in this position can give a different perspective than an expert.

Have you heard someone speak at a Q&A who was interesting and had insights that left you wanting more? If she was open to helping people by speaking at a Q&A, she may be open to helping you.

Find someone whose career just took off. When a person gets that big break, the tendency is to feel very excited and grateful. Sharing success stories can be a wonderful experience for both of you!

Do you know, or have you met successful people but not ever discussed business? Now's the time.

While you can simply ask for business advice, asking people to mentor you makes it a win-win situation. How many times have you heard award winners thank their mentors or read articles where the interviewees refer to what was learned from their mentors? When you ask for mentorship, you win because you get guidance and the mentors win because they get the opportunity to give back. It is an honor to be asked to mentor. Give people that honor.

When targeting mentors, be sure to have a range of people, as I mentioned earlier. It's like applying for colleges; be sure you have some "safe schools." In other words, have some people who you are pretty sure will say, yes.

What do you do once the people you ask agree to be your mentors? As learned in Week 8, when creating any new relationships you should ask questions to which you really need answers. Think of it as doing an interview or a documentary on how he got to where he is now. Really dig deep. If he says, "I was in the right place at the right time," or "I just got lucky," have him explain how he got to that right place or what he was doing before he got lucky. Sometimes, successful people don't realize how much they did to get to where they are, so it is your job to keep asking how.

Once you know how he did it, tell him where you are in your career, how you got to where you are now, and what you would like to be doing in five, ten, twenty years. Ask what you can be doing right now to get you on that track.

Be sure that before you end your conversation, you have concrete actions from all of your mentors. Take those actions. In your next conversation you can report on your progress and get further advice.

Mentor conversations can be very insightful, motivating, and valuable! They can help you through the hard times and remind you that there are people out there who care and want to help you.

In your journal, formulate a list of twenty potential mentors. Concentrate on whom you want to reach.

Later, we'll discuss how you will get to them. Be sure you have a list of people at different levels, including people you believe will say yes because you know them already or have a connection to them.

week 10
WORKING GIRL

T he corporate jungle at its worst and at its best, this comedy
follows Tess McGill's rise from secretary to businesswom-
an. When her boss breaks her leg, Tess takes over her office,
apartment, and wardrobe, determined to turn her big idea into
a big deal. Through it all, Tess makes smart decisions by doing
research to keep on top of her game.

One of the fears I hear over and over again regarding meeting new people is, "What will I say?" To overcome that fear, do
research on the person you're going to meet or on the company
you're meeting about. Research on entertainment industry people
is accessible on the Internet through sites such as *www.imdb.com*
and *www.google.com*. Just plug in the name of the person you're
researching. The credits and personal history will be there for the
accessing. Most production companies have their own Web site or
can be found on *www.hcdonline.com*, which is the online version
of the Hollywood Creative Directory that can be found at most
major bookstores.

Other places to research are the trades. The two big ones are
The Hollywood Reporter and *Daily Variety*. There are also trades

and magazines for specific classifications. For example, camera people can subscribe to *ICG*, *ASC*, and *SOC* magazines. They may also read *Below the Line*, a trade paper for people who work below the line. Check out the union Web site for whatever classifications you fall under. Simply put your classification into the Google search engine, for example, "Production Designers Guild" or "Writers Guild" and it will show you the union Web site. Unions are a great place to start when looking for contact information on someone. Their Web sites are also a great place to look for member interviews and articles.

When researching an individual, your objective is to find information that you can connect to or relate to or information that you have questions about. Fill in a bio sheet for each person you plan to meet so that you have enough information to start conversations, to make a connection, and to ask effective questions.

BIO SHEET

NAME: _____

Credit One: _____

Other Crew Members: _____

_____

_____

_____

Outstanding Scene One:_____

_____

_____

_____

Outstanding Scene Two:_____

_____

_____

_____

Credit Two: _____

Other Crew Members:_____

_____

_____

_____

Outstanding Scene One:_____

_____

_____

_____

Outstanding Scene Two:_____

_____

_____

_____

Other Credits: _____

_____

_____

_____

_____

Personal Interests/Facts: _____

_____

_____

_____

_____

Common Interests/Facts:_____

_____

_____

_____

_____

QUESTIONS:

1. _____

_____

2. _____

_____

3. _____

_____

4. _____

_____

5. _____

_____

Notes: _____

_____

_____

_____

_____

If you are researching a specific show that you would like to work on, you want to find out the names of as many people involved with the show as you can. Once you have them, you can share the list with the people on your Contact List. Ask for referrals to the people they know on your list. I will discuss referrals in Week 15, but for now, become familiar with the Show Breakdown. You can begin to compile the information on the shows you are interested in. You can find the information on shows in the trades *Hollywood Reporter* (Tuesday) and *Daily Variety* (Thursday), on IMDb, and many other production Web sites that you will find through Internet search engines.

SHOW BREAKDOWN

SHOW: _____

Network: _____

Production Co: _____

Phone #_____

Address: _____

_____

_____

Location: _____

EXP: _____

Co-EXP: _____

SUPR PROD: _____

PROD: _____

Co-PROD:_____

Line Prod: _____

Additional Writers:_____

_____

_____

_____

_____

_____

Director: _____

1st AD: _____

2nd AD: _____

Casting Director: _____

Director of Photography: _____

Production Designer: _____

Editor: _____

Actors:

_____

_____

_____

_____

_____

_____

Miscellaneous Crew:

_____

_____

_____

_____

_____

_____

_____

1. Do a bio sheet on five people on your mentor list.

2. If you are interested in working on specific projects, do a show breakdown for three of them.

week **11**

BIG FISH

T his movie revolves around a son who is trying to learn more about his dying father by piecing together the stories he has been told over the years. The stories of Edward Bloom's life are delightfully whimsical and entertaining, so much so that his son can't tell reality from myth.

How fascinating to have been in the presence of Edward Bloom, to have listened to tales of his magical life. He had stories about his work, friends, and the one woman who captured his heart. Could you be an Edward Bloom? What are your stories?

Have there been times when you were given referrals from friends or colleagues and before calling wondered, what will I say to them? Or why would they want to talk to me? Like Edward, you are unique. The way to connect with new people is to share the highlights of your life. A highlight is any moment that brought you joy or sparked your passion. People are drawn to passion—share yours!

Stories are the foundation of the entertainment industry. People are in this business to tell stories. They write them, act them out, direct them, design their backgrounds, and reveal them with lighting. Some people tend to the details of the clothing, the hair

55

and makeup, and the food design. In whatever aspect they contribute to a project, their common goal is to tell the story.

Knowing this, the best way to connect to storytellers is through swapping stories. If your first thought is, "But I haven't won an Oscar or worked with Julia Roberts," then I suggest you give yourself a break. After all, if you had won an Oscar, you would already be well known. People simply want to find out where you are on your journey and what's been great about the ride so far. You will find this skill to be very important when we deal with networking in Week 23.

WHAT'S YOUR STORY?

Write five career highlights.

Highlight One:_____

_____

_____

_____

Highlight Two:_____

_____

_____

_____

Highlight Three:_____

_____

_____

_____

Highlight Four:_____

_____

_____

_____

Highlight Five:_____

_____

_____

_____

Write five personal highlights. If after an hour you really can't come up with any, feel free to ask friends and family what they feel makes you unique.

Highlight One:_____

_____

_____

_____

Highlight Two:_____

_____

_____

_____

Highlight Three:_____

_____

_____

_____

Highlight Four:_____

_____

_____

_____

Highlight Five:_____

_____

_____

_____

Another great way to connect with people in the industry is to talk about the moment when you knew this was what you wanted to do. Everyone has such a moment. For example, here is mine:

I was five years old, watching my favorite television show, The Monkees, *when I saw a little girl talking to my favorite character, Mickey. I was so amazed that Mickey was talking to this young girl (who wasn't me) that I had to know how she got there. I immediately called for my mother who came running to my room. When I asked her how that girl got to talk to Mickey, she explained that she was an actress. It was that moment that I knew I had to be an actress, too!*

For some people it was a complete and overwhelming passion when they discovered costumes, cameras, and construction. For others, they simply stumbled upon their career when asked to tag along to a set by a roommate who needed someone to move sandbags on a freebie film. Others got into the business for the money. They may recall reading an article about a small independent film that went on to gross millions.

Talking about something you know instills confidence. Sharing your stories gives you connection to the people you meet.

In your journal or on your computer, create a section/file called: My Life Stories. Every time you have a career or life highlight, write it down.

YOU'VE GOT MAIL

While a small bookstore owner clashes with a large bookstore chain owner who puts her out of business, she finds love online with none other than her nemesis, Joe Fox. Kathleen Kelly may be devastated about the loss of her store, but she is uplifted by the relationship she creates through the exchange of e-mails.

E-mails are effective in business, too. That said, for me, in this day and age of e-mails, it is such a gift to receive a personal note in the mail.

The great thing about writing a letter is that you can carefully choose what you want to say. Crafting a note will introduce you in the best possible light.

When approaching someone for the first time, a telephone call isn't necessarily the most effective way because the person on the other end can get caught up in a mental conversation: "Who is this? What did he say his name was? John told him to call me? Huh. I wonder how John is doing. Last time I spoke to John he was working on his golf game. I need to work on my golf game…" and suddenly the person has missed every word you said.

With a letter, a person can take the time needed to read and understand who you are, what you want, and why you want it from him.

In Week 9, you made a list of mentors you were interested in obtaining. Writing a letter to each of them is a great way to introduce yourself. Here are the four essentials to writing an effective letter:

1. In the first paragraph, start with an introduction about who you are, what you do, and what you want to be doing. The first paragraph is also a good place to mention a referral from a mutual colleague/friend if you have one.

2. In the second paragraph, write about what you want from this person. Be sure to evaluate if you are requesting something to which he can say, yes.

3. The third paragraph is where you express why, out of all the people in this industry, you have chosen him to advise and guide you. It is very important that you do your research to clarify what it is that you value and what he can teach you.

4. Finally, you have to let him know how to contact you and how you plan to follow up. Whenever possible, you want to keep the ball in your court. Write that you will follow up by giving a specific date to expect your call. To get a follow-up number you can search the Internet, call the unions, or approach a mutual contact. If these methods fail, you must indicate in your letter how *you* can be contacted at his convenience.

Here are two sample letters:

Leight Meter
C/O BTL Agency
000 Wilshire Blvd. Ste. 100
Beverly Hills, CA 90210

Dear Mr. Meter:

I am a camera operator making the transition from independent to studio production. I have worked on a diverse number of projects independently, including Joe and Beth's Vacation *and* The Object *directed by Paul Thomas Anderville. Since joining the union, I am committed to working in the studio system.*

To achieve my goal, I am seeking out an expert, such as you, to give me career advice and guidance as a mentor. Understanding how busy your schedule is, I only ask for the opportunity to speak with you on three separate occasions for a minimum of ten-minutes each session. These can be either in person or by phone, over a twelve-week period at your earliest convenience.

I am a great admirer of the films you have shot (especially the eerie mood you created in Someone in the Shadows) *and the lengths to which you've gone to bring production back to the United States. I see that you have eighty-four IMDB credits, which tells me that you are very successful in navigating through the Hollywood system. It would be such an honor to learn from you. I know that any guidance you would be generous enough to provide would be invaluable as I begin this journey.*

You can contact me at 555-1212, or I will call you on January 17th for your response.

Thank you.

Sincerely,
Joe Camera

◂ ◂ ◂ ◂ ◂

Barton D. Rector
333 Spielberg St.
LA, CA 90046

Dear Barton,

Last month I attended a screening of The Wolf Lives *and listened to you speak. I was the girl in the front who asked you if your use of light was reflective of the wolf's fear of fire. You said yes and to wait for the DVD because you had a lot more to reveal about the carefully selected choices you made. I can't wait. I'm captivated by your work!*

I am about to direct my first short. I've produced a sitcom pilot, starred in various independent films, and written scripts. Directing is a new exploration for me. Wanting to be as prepared as possible, I am respectfully requesting that you be my mentor during this time. I understand how busy your schedule is; I

Jessica Sitomer

only ask for the opportunity to speak with you on three separate occasions for a minimum of ten-minutes each session. These can be either in person or by phone, between now and May.

I am a great admirer of Hurricane (to this day I won't go out in a storm) and The Underachievers (at which my conservative parents laughed out loud). Seeing your films has inspired me to be creative with angles, to light for suspense, and to think about how many ways to shoot two people having a conversation. Listening to you speak revealed that you are outgoing, passionate about what you do, and knowledgeable. I know there is so much I can learn from you!

Thank you for your consideration. Your time and advice would be greatly appreciated. You can contact me at 323-555-1212, or I will call you on March 19th for your response.

Best wishes,
Lila Bivens

The letters are guidelines for you to use. Be sure to personalize every letter to make it your own. Make it conversational when it applies and professional when it applies. Have someone, whose opinion you value, give you feedback on your letters. Things to check before sending your letters:

• Does your letter honestly represent you? Don't lie about your credits, experience, or personal history.

65

- When including a referral, be sure to have permission from the person whose name you are using.
- Can your letters be differentiated from each other? If you can just switch the name of the addressee, then you are sending a form letter.
- Is your letter 100 percent positive? This is no time to let any deep-seeded feelings of bitterness, envy, or desperation surface. People want to be around vibrant, passionate people; therefore, focus on what makes you vibrant and passionate.

This is your first impression—make it stand out!

Write a letter to one person on your mentor list, and give it to someone whose opinion you value for feedback. Once you have a letter that is ready to send, write two more. One of your three letters should be to someone you feel will say yes.

Note: You will not send the letters out until Week 14.

INVINCIBLE *13*

B ased on the true story of Philadelphia Eagle Vince Papale, *Invincible* finds Vince at the low point in his life. He's out of work, and his wife has left him. An open tryout for the Eagles creates the opportunity of a lifetime for Vince and a cruel note from his wife provides the motivation to succeed.

What drives you? The driving force is the force that motivates you. Along your career path you will have inspirational moments of achievement, but you may also experience monumental disappointments. You need to look inside yourself to find out what motivates you in your career. It's knowing this that will get you through making a difficult phone call or going to a networking event when you would rather stay home and watch television. It's motivation that will push you to approach experts, to overcome fear, and to find solutions to the challenges you will face as technology and methods change.

When you key into why you're passionate about your career path, it motivates you to continue learning, to stay immersed in your field, and to surround yourself with positive people who challenge and inspire you to follow your dreams.

How do you stay focused on your goal when you are met by obstacle after obstacle the way Vince was? You stay focused on your positive driving force.

Motivation and drive are different for everyone. It can come from anything that excites you, moves you, or makes a difference to you. However, there are positive driving forces and negative ones. A positive driving force means you are motivated by something positive. If you want to get a job because you *don't* want to lose your benefits, that's coming from a negative place. A negative motivation means you're motivated by a negative emotion or something you don't want. If you look at Vince, he had a negative drive for most of the movie: the note he had from his wife telling him he would never amount to anything. This negative drive got him far enough to make it on the team. Yet, it wasn't motivation enough for him to become all that he could be. Wanting to prove his wife wrong, the drive was coming from a negative place of hurt, anger, and betrayal. When his coach told him to, "Do it for the fans," Vince's motivation shifted to a positive one. Suddenly, he was driven by the desire to give them a win so the fans could feel good. It was this positive motivation that pushed him to be his very best.

To determine what motivates you, try this simple exercise:

Think of three moments in your career when you achieved greatness or moments that filled you with pride. Be sure they're moments when you felt great. What was it about those moments that filled you with pride? Write about why they made you feel so great:

Moment One: _____

_____

This moment felt great because: _____

_____

_____

_____

Moment Two: _____

_____

This moment felt great because: _____

_____

_____

_____

Moment Three: _____

_____

This moment felt great because: _____

_____

_____

_____

Analyze these three moments to look for a common theme. What did they all have in common? Did they all give you the opportunity to do what you love about your craft? Did you enjoy the research and homework that allowed your creativity to shine? If so, perhaps the theme is creativity.

Maybe your theme is family, fun, freedom, or wealth. Turn that theme into a motivation. For example, if you're theme is family, you can turn it into a motivation like this: I am motivated by the desire to provide a great life for my family.

Remember to check your motivation to be sure it's coming from a positive place. Note the negativity of these two statements: I am motivated by the desire never to have my family want anything I can't give them. I am motivated by the desire to be financially successful so that I will never be broke.

1. Write your positive motivation statement.

I am motivated by the desire to_____

_____

_____

2. Accomplishing my career goals will mean/yield:

1._____

2._____

3._____

WALL STREET

G ordon Gekko takes young, ambitious stockbroker, Bud Fox, under his wing, mentoring him on how to be successful on Wall Street. Gekko teaches his philosophy that "Greed is good," and advises Fox on how to make it in the world of the rich and powerful.

One lesson you can learn from *Wall Street* is to be mindful of whom you choose as a mentor. Bud wound up in a world of trouble learning from Gordon. Another lesson is "Mentors are good," in regard to learning. These are the steps to a successful mentorship:

1. Research the people whom you want to be your mentors.
2. Design questions for your mentors based on what you want to know and what you've learned about them. It is important to design your questions *before* you approach them. This is because some people are so honored to be asked that they call you sooner than you expect. You want to establish right off that you are professional and prepared.

   If you find yourself in a position in which a mentor calls and you are unprepared, say you recognize how valuable his time is and would like to reschedule. Tell the mentor that, in this way, you can have prepared questions available, making better use of the time being offered.

3. Introduce yourself with letters. (Personalized to each mentor.)

4. Follow up if you don't hear from them.

5. Schedule your first meetings.

6. During the first meetings, listen carefully for active tasks that you can do before your next meetings. Before leaving, sum up the tasks you've gleaned from the conversations. Ask if there is anything else they can recommend you do. If you are unable to determine any active tasks from your conversations, before you adjourn, ask your mentors for three tasks to work on during the month. Should this be difficult for them to do, ask them to recall when they were in your present position. Knowing what they know now, what would they have done differently? Be sure to leave with at least one task; it is vital to the mentor process. Make note of your mentors' family names, pets, hobbies, and other important personal subjects.

7. Schedule your next meetings.

8. Send a thank you note for the meetings.

9. Spend the month doing your best at accomplishing every task given to you.

10. During the second meetings, repeat to your mentors what they advised you to do. Share your results. Ask more questions and get new active tasks to work on for your next meetings.

Get to know more about your mentors on both a professional and personal level.

11. Schedule your next meetings.

12. Send a thank you note for the meetings.

13. At your third meetings, discuss your month's achievements, how the tasks they gave you worked out, and your ideas on how to maintain the momentum. Ask for your mentors' feedback on your future plans. When the meetings are over, thank your mentors for their time, and reiterate how valuable it has been for you to work with them. Remind them that their commitment of three conversations has been fulfilled. At this point, you can request to stay in touch with your mentors to keep them informed of your progress.

14. Send a thank you note for the meetings.

Designing questions for your mentors is extremely important. The quality of your questions indicates where you presently are in your career. Ask questions that reflect your time and experience in the business. Only ask questions to which you really want answers. It is all right, even recommended to ask questions that you think you know the answers to in order to get other opinions.

Here are some sample questions:

1. How/where did you get your start in entertainment?

2. What movies/TV/music videos/documentaries/commercials inspired you?

3. When did you know this was what you wanted to do?

4. Where did you start in your career? Did you expect to be here at this time? What do you still hope to accomplish?

5. How did you make the transition from _____ to the next level? What business tools did you use for this transition (calls, set visits, mentors, etc)? Were any of them especially difficult for you but worth it in the end?

6. Did you take projects that you didn't like just to work? What did you learn from the experience? Are there red flags I should be aware of?

7. Knowing what you know now, if you could start over, what would you do differently? What mistakes might I avoid making?

8. What have been your major ups and downs? How might I prepare for them?

9. Because everyone has his or her own way of doing things, what do you look for in a _____ (your classification)?

10. I'm sure you get countless "I'm available" calls. What calls have stood out and gotten a call back, and why? Have you ever returned a cold call? If so, have you ever hired a cold caller?

11. How do you feel about giving referrals? How do you feel about asking for referrals?

12. What were the relationships that made the biggest impact/difference in your career? How did you form them?

13. Have you ever been mentored? How did that relationship affect your career?

14. What advice can you give me on creating new relationships with people in our industry?

15. This is what I've been doing to advance my career_____. Knowing the state of the industry, what more can I be doing that I haven't thought of yet?

16. How do you stay in the loop when you're working on a long-term project?

17. What is your relationship with your agent? What is the most effective way to make use of that relationship? Do agents have tools that, if I had access to them, would benefit me? How much involvement does your agent have?

18. How much do you rely on your_____ (other classifications)?

19. Do you prefer to collaborate on projects or follow a strict plan?

20. Where do you go for other sources of creative outlet?

21. I am making the transition from _____ to _____ what skills/tools might I be unaware of that I need?

22. Where should I invest my time and money first? Where should I not invest my time and money?

23. Do you recommend any entertainment organizations? Watering holes?

1. Formulate five questions (these can be the same as the ones from Week 8, or you may have new questions).

1. _____

   _____

2. _____

   _____

3. _____

   _____

4. _____

   _____

5. _____

   _____

2. In Week 12, I had you write three mentor letters. This week you will send them out.

GLENGARRY GLEN ROSS

*G*lengarry Glen Ross portrays the high-pressure world of real estate sales, where the good sales leads only go to "closers."

Leads are to salesmen what referrals are to entertainment industry people. With everything on the line (money, reputations, jobs) people don't want to hire someone they don't know. Here's another Hollywood catch 22: how do you get to know the people who won't meet you if they don't know you? You get to know them through the people you already know. In other words, you get a referral from a mutual acquaintance.

Referrals are defined as:

1. having relation or connection
2. directing attention, usually by clear and specific mention

So many people in our industry waste valuable time and energy making cold calls.

Cold Calls are defined as:

> 1. Telephone calls soliciting business made directly to a potential customer without prior contact or without a lead

Here's why I say you're wasting valuable time making cold calls: cold calls work only 0.01 to 8 percent of the time. The number of calls you'd need to make to get a payoff is not an effective use of your time.

Here's why I say you're wasting valuable energy making cold calls: most people despise making them and spend a great deal of energy worried and upset over having to make them.

If you're someone who doesn't like making phone calls, a referral can boost your confidence because it creates an instant connection with a stranger. You become the mutual friend or associate. See more on handling "fear of phones" in Week 24.

Ask all the people on your Contact List for referrals. Be clear that you're *not* asking for a recommendation. This would mean putting their reputation on the line by saying that you are the best person for the job. Although, it would be fine if they offered to give you a recommendation, you are simply asking to use their name as an introduction so when you call the new person, you are not calling cold, you are calling with an introduction from a mutual acquaintance. If you know someone your contact should meet, offer to trade referrals.

You can ask for referrals to get introductions to the following:

- People with job opportunities
- Other guild members
- Mentors
- Other people in the entertainment community
- Production companies
- Entertainment organizations
- Agents and managers

The more specific you can be about whom you want referrals from, the better. Share your Target List, and if the people don't know anyone on, it ask them if they know people who are in the same classification as the people on your Target List.

When requesting the referral, ask for an introduction to be made, a call on your behalf, or *permission* to use their name. If they plan to make the introduction, or call on your behalf, ask when you should follow up with the person who said they are going to make the call on your behalf. You want to follow up with them to see if they made the call and how you should proceed. It's important to remain on top of the situation.

Once you receive referrals, you shouldn't wait more than a few days to call the person you were referred to. The contacts who gave you the referrals may be so excited they call their acquaintances to tell them to expect your call. If you wait too long, the acquaintances may think you're unreliable.

When you call your referrals, design a strategy for your calls. Know what your objective for the call is before you make it so you'll know when you've achieved it. Here are possible reasons for your calls:

+ Setting up an informational interview
+ Asking for advice
+ Inviting them to a screening
+ Asking them about work they've done on a specific project that applies to something you're currently working on
+ Getting feedback on your marketing tools

Plan your request for follow-up in advance as well. Use, "This has been really helpful. If I have more questions in a month or so, may I call you again?" If they say, "Yes," write it in your book to call them in a month. Or, "I appreciate your watching my reel. May I call you for feedback in two weeks?"

Use this template for your calls to keep you sharp. It will help you to feel prepared and focused on what you want. If you can't check off that you achieved your objective as the call is ending, be sure to ask for what you want, even if it's a follow-up to discuss what you didn't have time to talk about in the initial call.

CALL OBJECTIVE SHEET

NAME _____

Referred by: _____

Date of contact: _____/_____/_____

OBJECTIVE: _____

_____

_____

   Objective completed: _____

Results: _____

_____

_____

_____

Strategy for follow-up: _____

_____

_____

_____

Follow-up date scheduled for: _____/_____/_____

Keep track of the referral calls you make and the results. You can use the following template or create your own system for organizing your work.

REFERRAL PHONE LOG

Date: _____/_____/_____

Person called: _____

Referral received: _____

Referral's phone number: _____

Results: _____

_____

_____

_____

Follow-up date: _____/_____/_____

Referrals are the best way to meet the people you want to know. Using a mutual friend's name when contacting a person you don't know makes the whole process easier. Focus on meeting your friend's friends, making it about *friendship* not work, and you will find referrals to be an extremely valuable business tool!

and...*Action!*

1. Ask five people on your Contact List for three referrals.

2. Use the Bio Sheet from Week 9 to research your referrals.

3. Fill out a call objective sheet before each call.

4. Call all of your referrals.

5. Schedule your follow-up with each person with whom you choose to continue building a relationship. You can ask if it would be okay to call if you have any questions in the future; if the answer is yes, mark your calendar to call back with a question in a month. Or you can mention your plan to take action on one of their suggestions; tell them you'll let them know how it turns out.

Note: Be sure to follow up on the letters you sent last week if you haven't heard back.

LITTLE MISS SUNSHINE

Olive is a little girl with a big dream of winning the Little Miss Sunshine Pageant. To achieve this, her entire family bands together in a VW van to make the trip to California. When they hit obstacles, they have to make requests to get what they want. Sometimes they are told, flat out, no! Other times people say, yes, and are willing to help. Olive never gives up!

To get what you want in your career you have to *ask* for what you want. It sounds simple, but many people have trouble asking for what they want/need to help their businesses along. The business term for asking for what you want is called making a request.

A request is defined as:
1. the act or an instance of asking for something
2. something asked for

Somewhere along the line in our industry, this business practice has been turned into the uncomfortable practice of asking for a favor.

A favor is defined as:

1. friendly regard shown toward another, especially by a superior
2. gracious kindness; *also*: an act of such kindness

Asking for a favor implies reciprocity—this is not so with a request. That is not to say that favors aren't done in this industry, they are. But, for the most part, if you want something, be professional and ask for it—no strings attached.

The challenge for people when making requests is accepting the results. Once you make your requests, understand that the replies can be to agree, to refuse, or to offer another possibility. If you can't accept no as an answer, you're making demands, *not* requests!

It's hard to hear it, but the key is to accept the no and to thank the people for their consideration. If you do this, you keep the door open for making requests of them in the future. If you ignore the no and try different tactics to get what you want, they will feel uncomfortable and may not return your calls in the future.

You might want/need to request the following:

+ Referrals to other guild members and/or people in entertainment
+ Referrals to mentors
+ Feedback on your material (reel, script, resume)
+ A meeting

+ Advice on obtaining your goal
+ A set visit
+ Their time or help with a project

When making a request, be specific. The clearer you are, the easier it will be to get a straight answer. When it applies, ask for something that has measurable results. If you want referrals, ask for a specific number. If you request feedback, ask that you receive it by a specific date.

> *"I request that you watch my reel by Monday."*
> *"I have a request. Do you know three sitcom directors to whom you can refer me?"*

A rule that I will refer to over and over is:
Ask for something they can say *yes* to.

Put yourself in their shoes and ask yourself if you would say yes to the request. You may even choose to use the Rule of Five:
Ask five people their opinions before making an important decision.

Write ten things you need to help you achieve your career goals:

1. _____

2. _____

3. _____

4. _____

5. _____

6. _____

7. _____

8. _____

9. _____

10. _____

For each number above, choose a person from whom you can request what you need:

1. _____

2. _____

3. _____

4. _____

5. _____

6. _____

7. _____

8. _____

9. _____

10. _____

For the ten people you listed, how well do you know them? Review your requests and ask yourself if they are something to which the people can say yes. If you are unsure, ask for the opinions of others.

If you have any fears attached to asking for what you want, ask yourself these questions:

1. What are your concerns about making your request? _____

_____

_____

_____

2. What are the possibilities if your request is granted? _____

_____

_____

_____

3. What is the benefit(s) to the person of whom you're making the request if she says, yes? _____

_____

_____

_____

To be motivated to make your requests, the possibility of you getting a yes must outweigh your concerns about making them. Also, remember people will benefit from helping you simply by enjoying the satisfaction of being able to "give back."

From your list of requests, choose three and make those requests
this week.

JAWS

A great white shark decides to feed on swimmers in the waters of the peaceful tourist town of Amity Island. Though concerns are raised by Police Chief Martin Brody, the mayor doesn't want to lose his tourism money and keeps the beaches open. Fear spreads quickly when an attack happens on Fourth of July weekend. If they don't kill the shark, no one will go to the beach.

If there is a shark in the water and you're afraid to go in, that is a rational fear. We are born with a fight or flight instinct. Common sense says if you fight a great white, you're going to lose. But what happens if your fight or flight instinct starts kicking in over making a phone call or going to an interview?

There are many fears that plague our industry: fear of success, failure, humiliation, rejection, change, and financial ruin. Sometimes it's hard to identify from where these fears stem. Start by identifying what triggers your fears.

What industry related actions trigger your fear?

1. Making a phone call to ask for work or help from:
   A stranger (cold call) _____
   A friend/colleague _____
   An industry family member _____

2. Introducing yourself to:
   A stranger _____
   An acquaintance who doesn't recognize you _____

3. Asking a question:
   At a trade show _____
   At a Q & A panel _____
   Of a stranger you overheard talking about
   a subject that interests you _____

4. Taking a meeting with:
   A stranger _____
   A friend _____

5. Writing a letter or e-mail to:
   A stranger _____
   A friend _____
   An industry family member _____

6. Pitching/showing:

    Yourself   _____

    Your project   _____

    Your reel/resume/picture   _____

7. Other:

    Auditioning   _____

    Interviewing   _____

What other pre-job, post-job, or on-the-job triggers are you aware of that may not be listed above?

    1. _____

    2. _____

    3. _____

    4. _____

    5. _____

Identifying where your fears are coming from is the first step. Unlike the threat of a shark in the water, any triggers you checked off above are not a physical threat to you. There is no logical reason for your fight or flight instinct to kick in. Unfortunately for many, that doesn't mean it won't.

How do you halt the fight or flight instinct (that can stop you cold in your tracks with fear) that keeps you from taking the actions that will catapult you to success?

If the trigger puts you in such an intense emotional state that you can't work through your fears on your own, you may strongly want to consider talking to someone professionally.

The tools I will give you in this chapter are geared toward interrupting the patterns that you've created for yourself.

Imagine a river that flowed in one direction until one day a huge boulder landed in it, sending water in a new direction onto the soil. If that boulder remains, the river will continue to branch out onto the soil creating a deeper and deeper groove until it's a permanent stream.

That's how fearful thoughts work. One day you're going about your career business (the river), making a simple phone call, when you get something you didn't expect—a nasty, rude person on the other end (the boulder). This person tells you all the reasons why you can't have, do, or be what you want. You're devastated! You consciously or unconsciously choose not to make phone calls for a while. A few weeks later, you receive a referral from a friend. You sit down to make the call only to find yourself overcome with dread/fear/angst (the stream). The more times this happens, the deeper your fear of making phone calls.

Here's how the pattern works: You have fearful or negative *thoughts* about your career business. They create fearful negative *feelings* that stop you from taking the necessary *actions* to reap the results you want.

You *must* interrupt the pattern. I'm about to give you some exercises to interrupt the pattern from the moment those negative and fearful thoughts start popping up to torment you.

Some of the exercises may seem silly, but that's the point. The second you start thinking, "Boy I sure feel silly," you've stopped thinking, "I think I'm going to have an anxiety attack if I go to this meeting." These exercises are designed to make you feel anything *but* fear. I suggest you do the exercise when you're not in a state of fear. Your mind will be clear and you can formulate actions to take when you need them. Knowing you have these tools to access will help you feel prepared and ready to overcome your fears. Here are the exercises:

Change your emotion in a big way.

1. Choose an emotion that you would rather feel than fear (examples: joy, excitement, confidence):

   _____

2. What is a situation that would make you feel this emotion? If I... _____

   _____

   _____

3. Close your eyes and imagine you're in the moment, living that situation that makes you feel _____.
   Where are you? Whom are you with? What do you see, hear, smell, feel, taste? As you visualize, imagine what it takes to get you to the peak of your desired emotion.

When you've completed this exercise, I want you to notice that you were feeling that emotion because you were focusing on the thoughts that led you to the desired emotion.

When you are experiencing fear, it's because you are focusing on the thoughts that trigger fear. Have a couple of these emotionally driven situations thought out. When you sense fearful thoughts upon you, you can change your focus to a situation that will change your thoughts and emotions in a big way.

Excitement is one of the easiest emotions with which to interrupt fear because physiologically, the same things are happening in your body. Do the above exercise with something that would completely excite you to the point that you're jumping up and down and cheering. That's changing your emotion in a big way!

Be absurd!

Here's an exercise where you get to be silly. If your objective is to interrupt the fearful thought pattern, what is something so absurd that if you were to do it, it would crack you up? For me, I sing my favorite Bon Jovi song "opera style." It sounds so ridiculous that I start laughing. Maybe you could start making farm animal noises at the top of your lungs (chicken, cow, sheep). You'll feel ridiculous, but it's better than feeling anxious, right?

What are five absurd things you can do to change your fearful emotional state?

1._____
2._____
3._____
4._____
5._____

Be willing to try these extremely absurd techniques the next time you feel fearful. What do you have to lose but fear?

Counter your fearful thought.

If you recognize a fearful thought that has become a pattern ("I'm getting to old for this," "People don't want to help me," "I'm not going to know what to say,") create a counter, empowering thought for when that fearful thought shows up.

Fearful thought _____

_____

Counter thoughts:

1._____

_____

2._____

_____

3._____

_____

Fearful thought _____

_____

Counter thoughts:

1._____

_____

2._____

_____

3._____

_____

Fear is a very crippling emotion for many people in this industry and not to be taken lightly. There's a great quote, "Successful people feel fear but act in spite of it." Fear may always be a part of your career path. Consider that sometimes when you really care about what you're doing, the fear comes from wanting it to work out and concern about the consequences if it doesn't. If you care about what you're doing, you have to commit to pushing through your fears to achieve the success you desire!

1. What is one action that you've been avoiding because of fear?

_____

2. What reward can you commit to yourself upon completion of your action?

When I complete my action of _____

_____ I will reward myself with

_____

_____

3. Take that action!

4. If your fears are crippling, make an appointment to talk to a professional to see what options are out there to help you.

ELECTION

When Tracy Flick of Carver High decides to run for class president, she creates an aggressive marketing campaign using buttons, gum, muffins, and posters hailing, "Tracy Flick for President! Sign up for tomorrow, today!" Tracy knows she has to get her name out there especially when she finds herself competing with popular varsity football player, Paul Metzler, and his vengeful sister, Tammy.

Tracy didn't have much competition, but in the entertainment industry, you can be competing with hundreds to thousands of people for a single job.

How do you start competing with that many people?

1. Find out what marketing materials are expected for your classification. Here are some examples:

- If you are an actor, you will need a headshot, resume, Web site, and a reel of your work. (Information on writing resumes is included in this week's topic.)
- Most other classifications will need a resume, a Web site, and a sample of your work (reel, book, etc.).

2. Take it one step further; do research on the marketing materials expected for your classification. Here are some examples:

+ You ask ten Steadicam operators how long their reels are. They tell you between three and five minutes. If your reel is thirty-two minutes, it is safe to deduce that you need to shorten your reel.

+ Investigate the latest trends. If people are sending out their reels on a DVD while you're sending yours on a VHS tape, you may be perceived as behind the times.

You want your marketing materials to fit into the expected mold. On rare occasions someone does something that starts a trend, but in most cases, standing out from the crowd makes you look unprofessional and inexperienced.

3. Get outside assistance with your marketing materials. Examples of these are:

+ Make a list of the types of people who might best assist you (photographers, Web designers, reel editors)

+ Meet with between five and ten people before making your decision. This may seem excessive, but this is your calling card. You want to be comfortable with the person with whom you'll be working.

+ Before your final decision, try to get references whenever possible to check that they are reputable. After reading these, ask yourself if you are genuinely excited about the quality of their work.

+ When you do meet, come prepared with questions and know what the deal breakers are.

If you have to spend a lot of time on this research, it is *so* worth it! Unless you have exceptionally strong relationships with all of the people who want to hire you, your marketing materials are what stand between getting a meeting and being shuffled off into a big pile (which could possibly be in a trash can).

In addition to time, you also have to spend money. Your marketing materials are not the place to seek out bargains and shortcuts. That's not to say you can't find a great deal on pricing. However, that deal should be backed up by talent, or it's going to cost you more than you think. This is your first impression; most of the time you have anywhere from three seconds to three minutes to make it.

4. Get feedback from industry professionals before you duplicate anything! Changes can be very costly.

To do the research in these four steps, contact the following:

+ People who are already successful at doing what you want to do
+ Those who hire people who do what you do
+ Agents representing people who do what you do

Note: I didn't put parents and friends on the list. Your family and friends have a perception of you that may have nothing to do with how you want to market yourself in this industry. Unless your family and friends are in the industry and can be unbiased, get your opinions from the people suggested above.

All of the people I suggested are in constant contact with your competition's marketing materials. Use my Rule of Five. You may find that if you ask five people for their opinions, they all give you the same advice. That's when your work is easy and clear. Most of the time, however, you'll find that everyone has a different opinion and many of them may seem valid. That's when you have to consider the people you're asking and how to weight their opinions before coming to your final decision.

In short, please understand that this entire industry is based on perception. Create a professional perception, and that's how you'll be seen. Follow all of the above steps to do the job right and to give you that all-important edge.

The most common question I get is how to do a resume for the entertainment industry.

Remember those hundreds, possibly thousands, of people who make up your competition? Well, they're also writing resumes! How do you give yourself the edge among the others? It's most certain that you don't want to give the resume reader any cause to pass yours up or to toss it in the trash.

Be sure to avoid long paragraphs that force the reader to seek the name of the person who hired you or the name of the project on which you worked.

There's really no reason to include dates. They either make you look "too old" or "too young." People "in the know" will have an idea of how long you've been in the business by your credits.

Don't list classes that may make you appear "green." If you're in a union, they assume you know your craft. Listing the training classes you took to get up to speed on new technology isn't necessary.

Pictures haven't any place on a resume. Actors are the exception; although, it isn't mandatory for them, either.

Stay away from lengthy resumes. One page is sufficient. If you're using small type with too much information squeezed onto a page, it's difficult to read. If you have too much information, list your most current and/or impressive credits. When you are pulled from the pile, they will most likely check you out on IMDb, where they will see your full list of credits.

There may be exceptions to the above suggestions you will discover when you do your research.

If you want to get the resume reader's attention, there are certain aspects that must be included. Most important, write your name, classification, and contact info at the top of your resume. Decide if it's necessary/safe to list your address.

List your credits for the classification you're submitting. If you're submitting for a union feature DP, you don't have to list your loader or editing credits from twenty years ago. They want to know how you qualify as an expert for your particular submission. There are exceptions to this. Sometimes your credits from another classification may give you credibility in the field in which you're applying. For example, if you were a gaffer or camera operator for ten huge union features but your DP credits are all non-union, the former proves that you know your way around a union set.

Show the category that applies to who hires you. In the sample, I use the category director, but if someone else hires you, you want that category listed.

Special skills that apply to your classification, foreign languages, and, in some cases, skills that may be interesting conversation starters are appropriate for inclusion. It's also impressive to list awards. Be sure they apply to your classification. Promote your film school experience especially those schools with a strong alumni presence.

You can see from the sample resume (on the following page) written for our industry that it is different from a typical business resume. Note the use of columns, which allows readers to quickly find what they're looking for; this is a key point because the person reading your resume will read many other submissions.

Your Name
CLASSIFICATION
Contact phone number(s)
Email address/Web page

FEATURES	PROD. CO.	DIRECTOR
Yum Yum	Yummy Films	John Dough
My Dog Riley	Biscuit Films	Jake E. Lee
The Lock	Lock Films	Leslie Locke

TELEVISION		
Here is Here	ABC Network	Jack Boate
Mountain Brothers	Paramount Pictures	Toni Shamboli
More City Stuff	USA Network	Jess Mess

COMMERCIALS		
Vicks	Cough Prods.	Ralph Raspy
IBM	Sleek Geek Prods.	K-E-O
Jaguar	Good Livin' Prods.	J. Nice

MUSIC VIDEOS		
Bon Rovi—*Rockin'*	Rockin' Prods.	Todd Neuman
Coal—*Shovel It*	Hard Rock Prods.	Adam Rock
Shmuelle—*Obey*	Royalty Prods.	King Kabu

AWARDS
Sundance Film Festival, Official Selection (Classification)

SPECIAL SKILLS
Helicopter, Car to Car—stunts, PADI certified, Army Special Forces

EDUCATION
USC Film School

Do research on your marketing materials.

1. If you haven't any marketing materials yet, begin your research, and continue doing the work it takes (over the coming weeks/ months) to create materials that give you an edge.

2. If you already have marketing materials, get feedback and based on this, make any changes you deem necessary.

week 19
THE ITALIAN JOB

When one of Charlie Croker's own men turns on him, murdering his mentor and stealing his team's gold, Charlie and his band of thieves create the perfect strategy to get revenge—and their gold.

In Week 3, I covered goal setting. Anytime you have a goal, you need an action plan or a strategy to make it happen. The detail, expertise, and timing that went into Charlie's strategy plan was extensive and precise. When pursuing your career goals, you must have a strategy in place that encourages specific actions and gives you measurable results. In this way, you can see if your actions are producing the desired results. If they aren't, you change your actions until you get the results you want. It's easy to work hard. I'm sure you can find many tasks to do in a day toward your career, but are you working *smart*? Are the tasks you are doing getting you to the result you want within the fastest possible time frame?

In Week 3, you set a goal for the week. Did you accomplish it? Go back to Week 3, and review the criteria for creating a goal. Create a goal for this week.

By _____, I will have or be:

(one week from today)

_____

_____

_____

_____

Looking at your goal, what has to happen for you to be able to accomplish that goal?

Let's say you're an actor and your goal is to meet one casting director who can bring you in for an audition. What has to happen for you to accomplish that goal? Work backward to figure this out: What must happen for me to meet a casting director?

One possibility is to phone everyone you know until you find someone who knows a casting director. Request a referral and make that call. Use your contact's name and set a date for a meeting or audition (if it's a time sensitive project).

Another possibility is to research places where you can meet casting directors and go there. You can find their offices (but be sure they accept walk-ins). Attend Q&As where they're speaking on the panel. Take workshops where they teach.

Once you find them, sign up for their classes and attend the Q&As. If you don't get to meet one-on-one, write a personalized letter saying you enjoyed their workshops or the information they shared at the Q&As was very valuable. In the letter, make a request to meet. Follow up with a call to their offices.

I will go into detail about balance in Week 26. For now, focus on how to balance and to strategize one week. Make a list of the ways you spend your 168 hours per week (Example: on your career, sleeping, with family, at the gym). Approximate the average amount of time you spent per week on each area during the past month:

How I spent my time   Hours/Week

_____   _____

_____   _____

_____   _____

_____   _____

_____   _____

_____   _____

_____   _____

Based on the amount of time you devoted to your career last month, list all of the different actions you took to move your career forward (Example: phone calls, letters written, meetings, events attended):

_____   _____

_____   _____

_____   _____

_____   _____
_____   _____
_____   _____
_____   _____
_____   _____
_____   _____

The following is a formula and a template to help you organize a strategy for your career goals.

Your week's goal:

_____

_____

_____

What actions must you take to ensure the accomplishment of your goal?

1._____   6._____
2._____   7._____
3._____   8._____
4._____   9._____
5._____   10._____

Based on the people you already know, who can help you accomplish your goal? (Contact List Week 5)

1._____ 6._____
2._____ 7._____
3._____ 8._____
4._____ 9._____
5._____ 10._____

Whom do your friends/colleagues already know who can help you accomplish your goal?

1._____ 6._____
2._____ 7._____
3._____ 8._____
4._____ 9._____
5._____ 10._____

What requests do you need to be making to accomplish your goal?

1. _____
2. _____
3. _____
4. _____
5. _____

Whom do you need to know to obtain your goal? (Target List Week 7):

Which categories of people can help you?

1._____ 4._____

2._____ 5._____

3._____ 6._____

Specific people:

1._____ 6._____

2._____ 7._____

3._____ 8._____

4._____ 9._____

5._____ 10._____

Action Plan (your "To-do" list):
Completed

1. _____

2. _____

3. _____

4. _____

5. _____

Calls I must make:	Phone Number	Done
1. _____	_____-_____-_____	_____
2. _____	_____-_____-_____	_____
3. _____	_____-_____-_____	_____
4. _____	_____-_____-_____	_____
5. _____	_____-_____-_____	_____
6. _____	_____-_____-_____	_____
7. _____	_____-_____-_____	_____
8. _____	_____-_____-_____	_____
9. _____	_____-_____-_____	_____
10. _____	_____-_____-_____	_____

Create an action plan book. Design a strategy for this week that is the shortest means to your end goal. Take actions and analyze if they are working, if not, find new actions. Keep re-evaluating your plans until you achieve your goal! Add a new action plan to your book every week.

Note: In Week 4, you made a business plan. Tie the weekly action plans into what you need to accomplish each month. These plans should be manageable. If you feel overwhelmed, re-evaluate your plan.

FAST TIMES AT RIDGEMONT HIGH

week 20

*F*ast Times at Ridgemont High intertwines the stories of angst-ridden high school students struggling to pass tests, hang out, and have sex. Mark Ratner has a goal, winning the heart of Stacy Hamilton. He turns to his mentor, Mike Damone, who educates Mark on "the attitude." During one very important strategy meeting, Mike shares with Mark his five-point plan in which Mark learns: "You never let on how much you like a girl... You always call the shots... Act like wherever you are, that's the place to be... When ordering food, you find out what she wants, then order for the both of you... Now this is the most important, Rat. When it comes down to making out, whenever possible, put on side one of Led Zeppelin IV."

Strategy meetings take the meetings I've referred to in past weeks to the next level. The Strategy Meeting Form (found in this chapter) is a great tool for getting the most from your meetings.

If you schedule a meeting with a colleague or a mentor over coffee to get business advice, there is a casual feeling. This is fine for deepening relationships. However, the approach may not reap the same answers that an official strategy meeting potentially yields.

117

A meeting becomes a strategy meeting once you pull out a form with your advisor's name on it; suddenly, things are official and your mentor is challenged to offer you the best information with which to fill your page. In addition, you can share your Target Lists, action plans, etc. When your advisor sees that you've done your homework, he is more inclined to help you and also has all your great homework on which to advise you.

The Strategy Meeting Form is a simple one that allows the person to brainstorm ideas and to share referrals to his contacts with you.

STRATEGY MEETING FORM

With: _____

Shared contacts (referrals): _____

_____

_____

_____

_____

Other advice/suggestions:

_____

_____

_____

_____

Brainstorming ideas:

1. _____ ☐
2. _____ ☐
3. _____ ☐
4. _____ ☐
5. _____ ☐
6. _____ ☐
7. _____ ☐
8. _____ ☐

Follow-up date: _____/_____/_____

To use the form, simply share your strategy plan with the person you're meeting; ask for any ideas he has to offer. This is called brainstorming.

Rule #1 for brainstorming:

You don't speak or give an opinion. You listen and take notes.

Rule #2 for brainstorming:

Never negate or disagree with the person's suggestion. After the meeting, review the suggestions to check off the ideas on which you want to work.

Rule #3 for brainstorming:

> If the person is giving you ideas that you've already tried, write them anyway. Imagine how impressed he'll be when you call the next day to say that you've done the work. One should never tell the individual that the ideas did not work.

By following these rules, you create an atmosphere conducive to the free flow of ideas. Sometimes the craziest, most ridiculous ideas can trigger a truly brilliant idea. If you shoot down those ideas, he may shut down completely and not give you advice again. Be open to what the person has to say. Maybe you'll even get a fresh perspective on an old idea.

1. Be sure your action plan is ready to share at your meetings.

2. Make appointments for three strategy meetings in the next month.

FOR LOVE OF THE GAME

As Detroit Tigers veteran pitcher Billy Chapel strives to pitch the perfect game, he reflects on his relationship with girlfriend, Jane Aubrey. Early in their relationship, Jane asks Billy if he loses very much. He tells her that he loses, that he's lost 134 times. "You count them?" Jane asks. "We count everything," Billy answers.

Baseball is a game of statistics. When you turn over a baseball card you can read them for yourself. Yes, sports are fun. It's a dream come true when you make it to the major league. But, like the entertainment industry, sports franchises are moneymaking businesses. If you don't have good statistics, you're off the team.

Think about the statistics of the people in our industry. What differentiates those on the A-list, B-list, D-list, and of course, the no-list? The more work invested in their career, the higher they go on the list. To be on your desired list, you must do the appropriate amount of work.

The Progress-Tracking Template in this chapter enables you to keep track of your business statistics. This will help determine if you are doing enough to produce the results you want.

121

In Week 19, I asked you to look at the difference between working hard and working smart. This template helps you evaluate how you're working. There are different ways to use it.

One way is to monitor the efforts of your productivity. If in ten years you want to be on the A-List, you have to be doing the groundwork that it takes to get there. Let's say you're making eight calls in a month. Do you think that's the same number of calls made by someone at the top of her field? To give you an idea, I know A-list agents who roll eight calls at a time.

Monitor categories that reflect your classification and move you closer to your goals. (Examples: days worked, networking events attended, reels sent, headshots submitted, new relationships created, set visits, referrals received, and hours toward benefits, etc.)

Another is to evaluate what it takes to accomplish a specific goal. When you want to accomplish it again, you'll know the amount of work required. You can use it to determine how much work is required to generate one day of work. If you need three days of work to qualify for your benefits, you'll know what you have to do. Or you can track how many phone calls are needed for a desired outcome.

The template helps you to examine overwhelm in conjunction with minimal results. If you find that you are overwhelmed because you feel you're doing so much and nothing is happening, you can use the template to gauge your output. When many frustrated people break down what they are actually outputting, they realize it's not very much. Yet, because a fear trigger paralyzed them, they didn't recognize they'd stopped doing work. Then they used up an enormous amount of energy focusing on how overwhelmed they felt.

This tool also helps overachievers, who mistakenly feel underproductive, acknowledge their work. If the outcome doesn't appear exactly as planned, overachievers tend to disregard the productive work they've done. They beat themselves up for not working hard enough. I've heard them express incorrect generalizations such as, "I had an awful month." "I didn't get anything done." Keeping track of the many small steps you take toward your goals, will make you aware of the amazing amount of work you've actually accomplished!

As noted earlier, use the Progress-Tracking Template to monitor categories that apply to your classification while moving you closer to your goals. Do the tallies on a separate piece of paper, add them up at the end of each week, enter your totals each week, and then total for the month.

SAMPLE PROGRESS-TRACKING TEMPLATE

Statistic	Week 1	Week 2	Week 3	Week 4	Total
Phone calls made	15	20	51	93	179
Sets observed	1	1	2	6	10
Referrals received	12	16	10	8	46
Networking events attended	1	2	2	3	8

PROGRESS-TRACKING TEMPLATE

Statistic	Week 1	Week 2	Week 3	Week 4	Total

Track your progress by making a copy of this chart or creating your own version on a computer. Fill out the criteria you want to track. Put the form somewhere you can see it (by your phone, on your desk, on your fridge).

I encourage you to use this tool each month.

THE 40-YEAR-OLD VIRGIN week 22

A ndy Stitzer is a really nice guy who has patiently waited a *really* long time, forty years to be exact, to find a really nice woman so that he can finally lose his virginity. When Andy goes on a date with Trish, they hit it off, but their patience is tested when they mutually agree to get to know each other with a "no-sex-before-the-twentieth-date policy." Because of the patience it takes for Andy and Trish to hold out, their relationship grows stronger; in the end their patience pays off.

Can you imagine wanting something to happen in your career so badly that it was frustrating you to no end? Have you paid your dues and just want your break already? Is that time right now? What if you knew there would be a payoff in the end, but you just had to wait for it? Trish knew the payoff was coming, so they were able to relax and enjoy each other.

Learning to embrace patience is an invaluable mental tool, and in our industry, a very necessary one. By embracing patience, you are trusting that you will one day have your payoff. In the meantime, enjoy the journey.

Are you going to give up, or are you determined to pursue your dream? Do you truly believe this is what you are meant to be doing? Do you have faith that if you keep taking steps toward your career, your dreams will become reality?

If you answered that you're not going to give up and that you have blind faith in yourself, you have two choices. Either you embrace patience or become increasingly more frustrated, angry, bitter, desperate, and depressed. Keep in mind the more you demonstrate these traits, the less people want to be around you, which means no work for you.

This is a good time to reaffirm the truth of that old adage, "Patience is a virtue."

How does patience show up or not show up in your life?

_____

_____

_____

_____

It's important to uphold what you deem necessary regarding your career. To determine your values, ask yourself why it's important that you do what you do. In other words, what do you value about having a successful career? Find ways to stay connected to your values. Acknowledge the individual steps (big and small) as you strive to make your dreams come true.

You must accept what you can't control. If your career goals are doable, recognize that you're going to need time, effort, and energy to see them to fruition. Focus on what you can do.

Put your focus on living in the moment. Instead of dwelling on your past mistakes and failings, focus on your next step. Don't worry about what you will become or how you will act in the future. Begin to live each day as a new opportunity.

Get yourself some perspective. Movies aren't made in a day. During production, there are setbacks and surprises. Careers have setbacks and surprises as well.

Before developing the skills needed to increase patience, identify the present state of yours.

Answer the following questions:

1. How patient are you with your rate of career growth? _____

_____

_____

2. What feelings do you experience when you are impatient? _____

_____

_____

3. What negative consequences have you experienced as a result of your lack of patience? (Example: Have you ever followed up too

many times because you were anxious about a job and then lost it?)

_____

_____

4. What beliefs block your ability to have patience? (Examples: I'm running out of time, or I'm too old.)

    1. _____

    2. _____

    3. _____

5. What replacement beliefs would help you gain more patience? (Examples: I have the rest of my life, or as long as there's someone else my age doing it, so can I.)

    1. _____

    2. _____

    3. _____

6. What new behavioral traits could you develop to gain more patience? (Example: I could say my replacement beliefs as daily affirmations, or I can take yoga.)

    1. _____

    2. _____

    3. _____

When you become impatient or anxious about wanting things to happen "your way," remember rushing results will make you miss the opportunities presenting themselves. You will miss the growth process that comes with the ups and downs of our industry.

Countless times, I have heard of experiences people perceived to be negative. For example, when looking back on missed opportunities, being fired, and burned bridges, people discovered they were blessings in disguise. The people who are able to say that it wasn't meant to be or that something better will come along have the "patient attitude" it takes to persevere in our industry.

Embrace patience in your career journey, so when your payoff comes, it will be a moment worth waiting for.

1. Examine how cluttered your life is with anger, resentment, and hostility in regards to how long it's taking to accomplish your goals.

2. Each time you see impatience show up, write an entry about it in your journal. Determine how you can be more accepting of the concept of "being patient along your career path."

week 23

PRETTY WOMAN

Edward, a successful businessman picks up Vivian, a hooker, to be his escort. In his position, Edward knows the importance of attending networking events. He goes to parties, polo games, and business dinners. Unlike Edward, who wants to form or to maintain relationships at the events, his date, Vivian, has nothing at stake. Therefore, she chats with various people whether they are kind or catty.

Almost all people in our industry have *no* problem talking to people who have nothing to do with the industry. However, the moment they know that the person to whom they are talking can hire them, they become shy, uncomfortable, and awkward.

I do a wonderful exercise. I ask a client to pretend that a friend has asked her to pick up his out-of-town guest at the airport because he's busy working. I assume the role of the guest, who is a teacher. I "get into the car" and see how the conversation goes. It always seems to flow freely with no questions about my career because she already knows I'm a teacher.

Eventually, we hit a lull in the conversation where the client, who let's say is a television writer, tries to break the silence. "So, you're a teacher."

To which I reply, "Yes."

She asks me what I teach. I tell her, "Writing for Television at NYU."

She asks, "Really? What's your name?" To which I respond with the name of a hugely successful television writer, such as Dick Wolf.

What happens next is always fascinating. It's as if I've suddenly morphed into a man and became Dick Wolf in this client's eyes. Usually the client's face drops, turning white. She has shortness of breath and begins stumbling on her words. This forces me to end the exercise, point out that I am not, in fact, Dick Wolf, and remind her to take some deep breaths.

I cite this exercise because this week's subject is the importance of networking. Before I discuss its necessity and value, I have to address the fear that engulfs so many people when I suggest they attend an event for the purpose of meeting people.

I hear many reasons why people don't like to network:

+ They are shy and/or don't know how to break the ice.
+ They perceive networking as schmoozing or phony.
+ They don't know what to say.
+ They don't want to be perceived as using people.
+ They don't know where to go to network.
+ They have people in their lives who don't like to go with them and/or are not supportive of them going.
+ They don't have enough time to go.

These reasons are simply limiting beliefs that have become obstacles. Limiting beliefs are general statements that you've turned into facts. By now you recognize that meeting new people is a necessity of our industry. If you want to be successful, you'll have to come up with solutions to help you break through your internal obstacles.

I will address each of the above individually beginning with shyness. Most people who tell me they are shy are generally comfortable with people they know. But when it comes to going on their own to a place where they have to meet new people, they feel shy. A solution for this obstacle is to review your Contact List. Find an outgoing friend to accompany you. Be sure to tell your friend your purpose for going to the event and ask her to "break the ice" for you. You may know someone outside of the industry who is very outgoing. As with *Pretty Woman*'s Vivian, when there is nothing at stake for the person, it's even easier to start conversations with people. If you are alone, a simple icebreaker is to ask people what brought them to the event. Another is to ask them what they do. They key is to write down at least five icebreakers before you go. This preparation will give you the confidence needed to start a conversation. You may consider asking your outgoing friends what they say to break the ice.

Not knowing what to say to people may have been an old stumbling block of yours, but after Week 11, you realize you have wonderful stories to tell. Talk about how you got into the business, your highlight moments, and what you want to achieve. Also, prepare yourself with questions to ask other people. Sometimes, it's better to talk less and listen more. If you are prepared with questions to ask and stories to tell, you will be on your way to a very successful networking event. This might be a good time to review Week 11.

Most people don't like schmoozing or being phony because they're aware of some sleazy people out there. But that doesn't mean that you have to be one of them. If you genuinely are looking for likeminded people and are being sincere, you are not schmoozing or being phony. You're simply creating new relationships. Should you come across a phony person who rubs you the wrong way, simply move on. There are many kind, passionate people with likeminded sensibilities at networking functions waiting to be met. To disregard them by buying into this limiting belief is unfair and detrimental to your career.

If you don't want others to think you are using people, ask yourself, are you? If not, and you are genuinely looking to create relationships, you're not using people. Just because they're in positions to hire you doesn't mean you're using them. Instead of focusing on what they are thinking about you, focus on what you think about them. Are they people with whom you have likeminded sensibilities? If that's what you're looking for, you will not be perceived as a user.

Not knowing where to go to network in this computer age is simply an excuse. If you are in a major entertainment city like Los Angeles or New York, finding networking organizations is much easier. The Internet is a great resource. Go to google.com or ask.com and put in keywords such as entertainment networking organizations and the closest major city to you. Look online for organizations like Film Independent, Independent Feature Project, and Filmmakers Alliance. These are some of the big ones. If you went to a film school, you could research any alumni communities. Many special interest groups have organizations such as Women In Film. Film festivals are another great place to meet people, especially if you live in a non-entertainment community. Research the festival by reading up on the films they've selected and the people who worked on them. You can plan a trip to the festival with a specific Target List of films to see and people to meet. Big film festivals are Sundance, Cannes, Tribeca, and Los Angeles Film Festival. In addition, many different countries/states have film festivals.

If your significant other (SO) doesn't enjoy attending events with you and then complains that you're going to them, you may find yourself in a difficult situation. Help your SO understand why attending these functions is a vital step in your career. Embrace your new perspective on networking and enroll your SO to join you by finding win/win situations. If your SO doesn't want to accompany you or if you don't want him/her to, you must find a way to gain support. Perhaps you can embrace something important to your SO that you're not particularly wild about.

Complaining that you don't have enough time is once again, nothing but an excuse—you must make the time! Using the tools

I've given you streamlines your workload, giving you all the time you need.

Do you have a limiting belief about networking that I did not list? Try to come up with a solution on your own. If you find it too difficult, share your obstacle with some friends to get their ideas on what you can do.

Remember to be patient with yourself. You've spent most of your life buying into these limiting beliefs, so it may take some time to undo them.

1. Research the entertainment industry community in your area. If you live in a town or state that doesn't have one, research the closest location that does.

2. In your journal, make a list of events that interest you. Depending upon how confident you feel, you can choose to join a networking organization this week. Or you can get all the information about joining so you're prepared to sign up before completing this program.

J ack Cates is a cop. Reggie Hammond is a convict. This is a great movie about two people who couldn't have liked each other less yet needed each other more, and who never expected to be on the same side, even for *48 HRS.*

Although reluctant to partner with each other, *48 HRS.* was a great example of partnership at its best. Partnerships can be the solution to overcoming many of the obstacles in your career, too.

Before discussing how to use this tool in the entertainment industry, let's look at the premise of "No man is an island" in the business world. Upon examination of a successful company, it's doubtful you'll find only one person at a computer. Even people with Internet companies have outsourcing and additional help.

This fact holds true when considering the successful A-list companies in our industry, as well. They have many people working with them: agents, managers, publicists, personal assistants, accountants, etc. Why should *you* feel that you have to pursue your career all by yourself?

Partnerships help eliminate fear, add fun, and create successful breakthroughs, thus, bringing you closer to your business relationships. To find possible partners, examine the relationships you have already created. You'll notice that you have chosen to nurture relationships with people for different reasons. You probably have confidants, people who make you laugh, people who inspire you, and people you can count on in a crisis. Look to everyone you know: family, friends, teachers, classmates, and neighbors. Only choose people who you know will be encouraging and supportive.

Consider these challenges that exist in your career, right now:

+ Do you have calls and "drop-offs" you need to make?
+ Do you have a networking event to attend?
+ Do you have an audition?
+ Do you have other tasks you procrastinate doing?

Partnership can help in various situations. If you hate making calls and have a very important one, phone a friend whose opinion of you matters to tell him that you are going to make a call. Contact your friend after the call has been made. This is called *accountability*. Accountability is the act of answering to someone else. It's what you would have if you were part of a successful company. Because you're not an employee in a company, it's important that you create this accountability for yourself because you are the boss of a company. Or, if the situation applies, find yourself a partner who will pretend to be your assistant and to make the call for you.

Use this technique in any situation that an A-lister would have an assistant making a call on her behalf. This solution gives the added cache that you are so successful you need an assistant.

Actors do something called "drop-offs" where they drop off their headshot at a casting office. Some offices are open to this and others aren't. Unfortunately, many actors can't find out which offices don't comply until they find themselves being told off by the casting director. This can be terribly damaging to the actor's psyche. But what if the actor asks a friend, who makes them laugh, to go along? The daunting task can turn into a hysterical adventure.

Last week we talked about the importance of partnership for attending networking events. You don't want to find yourself in the trap of standing with your partner in a corner, conversing with each other all night. Once again, you want to create accountability by telling your partner your numeric relationship goal for the evening. By saying your goal is to meet five new people at the event, it forces both of you to reach out.

If interviews or auditions make you nervous, ask a friend to drive there with you. She will keep your attention focused on something other than your nerves. Knowing that someone will be waiting for you can calm and empower you.

Suppose there are tasks begging for your attention yet you respond by procrastinating. It's time to take aim and "throw your hat over the fence." For example, you're a writer sitting at your computer, staring at a script. Do you suddenly have the urge to empty the dishwasher or to take the dog for a walk? Create a deadline for yourself. Call someone you respect and tell her you will have a script ready by a specific date. Knowing your relationships with the people on your Contact List, use your common sense. Choose someone whose opinion of you matters, but whose opinion would not have negative repercussions on your career should you not make your deadline. In other words, ask another writer you respect, not a development executive who is interested in your ability to make deadlines.

What are three challenges you want to work through?

1. _____
2. _____
3. _____

Who are three people you can partner with in order to help you work through your challenges?

1. _____
2. _____
3. _____

How can your partners help you? What function will they serve? For example, if your challenge is meeting five people at a networking event, your partner's function will be to act as "the ice breaker." Once the ice is broken, you'll be able to partake in the conversation and create a new relationship. Do you need more assurance before asking a partner to help? Figure out what's in it for her to create a win-win situation. Maybe your friend needs to meet new people too and doesn't know about the event. Or maybe she feels good when helping other people.

This week, give yourself the gift of partnership. Allow yourself the joy of experiencing new things. Let the people you care about help you throw away old burdens.

Pick a challenge to work through. Who would make your ideal partner? Call that person. If he is unavailable, choose someone else. Keep asking until you find your partner.

I want to _____

_____

_____

My ideal partner would be _____

SCHOOL OF ROCK

*I*n *School of Rock,* Dewey Finn is a guy whose dream is to be a rock star. His reality is that he hasn't got a band, cash, or a job. When he poses as a substitute teacher, his way of reaching the students is through what he knows best: music. He forms his own band with the class of elite elementary school students who he believes can help him win the Battle of the Bands, solve his cash problems, and put him into the limelight.

In the nineties, I was inspired by Vince Vaughn and John Favreau and of course Matt Damon and Ben Affleck, who wrote their own vehicles. I found a partner. Together we created a television sitcom for us to star in. We called up literary agents and were pleasantly surprised when they embraced our pitch, "We're looking to meet your writers who haven't been staffed before and who are willing to work for free to get the experience of working as staff writers on a sitcom." We received more than two hundred writing samples from agents ranging from small boutique to the Big Five. After many interviews we selected six staff writers.

When they completed our pilot, we cast it. Our sitcom was created around a bar, so we only needed one set when we performed our show live at the Improv in Los Angeles. This venue was chosen for its reputation. Our plan was to perform a new episode each month. The strategy was to create buzz about a "live sitcom."

The strategy was working. Studio execs and agents were coming. Just as it started to pick up steam, two greedy writers got ahead of themselves and convinced the rest that they should stop writing for free. This was a setback, but my partner and I took it in stride. We had a writer who understood that taking risks and making sacrifices are a part of getting ahead. He allowed us to use his script as the pilot.

With a few adjustments, it worked. A budget was created for the cost of shooting the pilot. After asking a lot of wonderful people to donate their skills, time, and equipment, all we needed was $20,000—which we did not have. Using outside-the-box thinking, we came up with the idea of asking one thousand people for twenty dollars each. It worked, and we completed our sitcom pilot

Yes, there are the obvious, standard routes whereby people go through the studio system and networks. But, until they're accessible, it's important to think outside the box to find a way to work on your craft.

When you think outside the box, you may hear many people tell you what you can't do. Don't let the naysayers get you down. If you are committed to your project, you will find a way. With today's technology and Internet showcasing, there are limitless possibilities for getting your work out there.

Another idea is if you have a movie that you want to get

produced, create a trailer or shoot a short from it to use as a calling card.

Short films are great vehicles for actors, writers, directors, producers, and all heads of departments. People will work on them to build their credits. They also offer the possibility for making connections to future paying jobs and referrals. Working on shorts is not only good karma, but if you have nothing else going on, you are getting the opportunity to work on your craft.

To prompt you to think outside the box, brainstorm these questions on your own or with your creative friends:

- What are some ideas for projects?
- What do I need to complete my project?
- Who do I know who can help me with my project?
- Where can I advertise for people to help me with my project?
- Where can I showcase my project?

Remember, artistic people are happiest when doing what they love. So you have to find creative ways to keep yourself fulfilled with the possibility of it leading to the next step.

One of the most important factors for enjoying the journey of your career path is to find ways to *live your passion*.

It is extremely empowering to do your own projects. See what ideas you can come up with this week.

What are three ideas for ways to use your creativity?

1. _____
2. _____
3. _____

Create a plan for an outside-the-box project.

THE FAMILY MAN

week 26

What if you woke up and discovered that your sports car and supermodel girlfriend had become a minivan and a wife? That's what happens to Jack Campbell, a prominent investment broker, who wakes up one morning to find himself in bed with his ex-girlfriend, Kate. Only now, she is his wife and they have two kids, a dog, and are living in the suburbs of New Jersey. After discovering what it is like to be *The Family Man*, Jack's priorities in life change dramatically.

Congratulations! Here you are at the halfway point of the year. I've had you completely focused on your career. Now that you've learned many tools and have an understanding of the time line for accomplishing different tasks, I want you to look at your life overall and how balanced it is. What are your priorities? When you focus so intently on one area of your life, the other areas can't help but suffer. This can make you feel off balance. It's especially detrimental if the areas you are focusing on are not in alignment with your priorities. For example, I had a client who worked extremely long hours in order to make a lot of money to give his family a certain type of lifestyle. Family was his number one priority, yet because of

147

the amount of time he spent working, he had no time left to spend with them.

I had another client who was so ambitious she wouldn't let anything get in the way of her career. Every waking moment was spent creating relationships and working hard to build her company. Whenever I would suggest taking some time off for self-care, she said that there would be plenty of time when her career was where she wanted it to be. Finally, her body gave out, leaving her weak and bedridden for months. She had to learn the hard way that health was her priority.

Look at the pie chart on the following page. With colored pencils, fill in each section of the pie according to how much of a priority each piece is right now, with ten being most of your time and zero being none of your time. Remember, it's how much of a priority you're making it now, not how much of a priority you would like it to be. Notice where most of your time goes. To what aren't you giving time? Where are you not spending time that you would like to be? Are you settling in any areas, rationalizing that it's okay when deep down you feel it's not? Do you feel powerless in any areas that you want to prioritize but worry what the consequences would be if you did?

What would life be like if you had your priorities in order? This is the first time we're looking at your life as a whole. It will be the starting point from which all change will come. As of this moment, if your primary focus has been on your career, have your relationships or health suffered because of it? Being aware that you need balance in your life is the first step to acquiring it. Once you recognize the areas where you have not been making any effort but wish to be, it's time to commit to trusting yourself. Trust that if you take a little time from your career goals to concentrate on your love life and/or your health, that your career won't suffer. We are meant to be balanced, which is why we do get sick if we push ourselves too hard. Instead of perceiving the time you're allocating to your new priorities as time lost, re-evaluate how you are working. Develop a more concise plan, thereby getting the same results with less effort. If you don't know how, seek advice from people who have well-balanced lives. The more people you talk to, the more ideas you'll get on how to have it all.

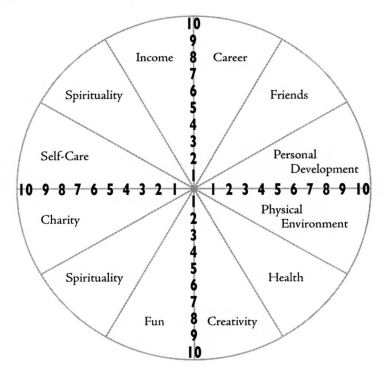

Choose three areas from the pie chart to which you would like to commit more time. Then take the first action. Whether it's planning a fun day, donating to a charity, or cleaning out a room, do it this week!

HOW STELLA GOT HER GROOVE BACK

S uccessful stockbroker Stella finds herself persuaded by her close friend to take a well-deserved first-class vacation to Jamaica. The beauty of the island and one particular young male inhabitant teach her the value of balance. Stella is forced to re-evaluate how to balance love, work, and motherhood.

This is the week where you will focus on self-care or, as I like to call it, the week of pampering. If taking a week to do this sounds like a waste of time, you'll just have to trust me. After you develop this wonderful habit of self-care, you'll be forever grateful.

Are you one of those people who have no problem pampering yourself? Then, go straight to step two. But, if you're one of those who feels guilty believing that your time and/or money should be spent solely on your career, start with step one.

To remove guilt and install the valuable habit of pampering yourself in its place, use the following steps:

1. Come to terms with your need for pampering. You don't have to feel guilty for taking care of yourself. This is a reward for all your hard work. It's soul nurturing as well as a communication to your

subconscious mind that you value yourself.

If you still feel that coming to terms with treating yourself is easier said than done, write all of the reasons you have for struggling with self-care:

1 _____

2. _____

3. _____

After reading this paragraph, close your eyes and think of someone you know who likes to indulge in pampering himself. Imagine this person is looking at your list of why you can't do this. What do you think the response would be to your reasons? What would he say to convince you that you're deserving?

2. I'll be asking you to make a list of all the ways you would like to pamper yourself. Don't worry about how you will be able to make them happen; simply list what you would like to do. Ways to give yourself the royal treatment can range from pricey to free.

Here's a sampling of suggestions:

+ Visit a health retreat
+ Go to a day spa
+ Get a facial or a massage
+ Take a yoga or meditation class

- Take a nap
- See an inspirational film
- Listen to a symphony
- Eat a great meal
- Travel (fly first class)
- Enjoy a fine wine
- Stay overnight in a hotel suite
- Go on a nature hike
- Spend a day at the beach
- Get a free makeover at a department store
- Take a bubble bath

When you write your list, be sure to include some treats that require short term commitments and those that are free or low cost. This will take care of any excuses!

MY PAMPERING LIST

1. _____ ☐
2. _____ ☐
3. _____ ☐
4. _____ ☐
5. _____ ☐
6. _____ ☐
7. _____ ☐
8. _____ ☐

Periodically, return to the list and check the box of each item/ action in which you indulged.

The first year I committed to making pampering a must in my life, I didn't have enough money to go to luxury resorts or to get massages. Instead, I indulged in lavender-scented bubble baths with candles. A few months later my sister's company rewarded her with a trip for two to a luxury resort in the Caribbean for herself and a guest. I was her guest. We had a beautiful beachfront room, with gourmet meals, and massages. Where there's a will there's a way. You will either figure out how or it will reveal itself.

3. Create a Pampering Must. For the next seven days, schedule one pampering action daily.

Schedule your Pampering Must into your calendar and enjoy!

THE GODFATHER

Michael Corleone, son of Mafia Don Vito Corleone, returns from WWII to get sucked into a life of crime, of which he has wanted no part. The story reveals people who betray his family or who won't do what the crime family demands of them. These people, even when family, are "eliminated."

You have learned about creating relationships, getting out there, and meeting new people. It's time to evaluate your existing relationships. Are there people in your life who are draining, discouraging, or making you feel bad in any way about you pursuing your dreams?

Since you are doing so much work physically, mentally, and emotionally, you deserve to be acknowledged and encouraged. However, you may find you have certain people in your life who don't make you feel good. They may show up in different forms:

- The Non-Supporters (NS): These are the people who, no matter how hard you work and how much you accomplish, never give you credit, compliments, or encouragement.
- The One-Uppers (OU): These are the people who, no matter what you accomplish, have done something better.

- The Physical Drainers (PD): These are the people who are always asking you to do things but never reciprocate. The PDs will call you even when they know you have a big meeting or a deadline to help with one of their "crises."
- The Mental Drainers (MD): These are the people who are always in need of two-hour advice conversations, yet they never take your advice. The MDs may call over and over on the same topic until you tell them what they "want to hear," which you can't very well do.
- The Not-So-Expert Experts (NSEE): These are the people who pick apart everything you're doing because they think they know better and have all of the answers (which they don't).
- The Crashed and Burned (CB): These are the people who've tried to do what you're doing, failed, and given up, and now they tell you why you can't do it.

Make a list of the people in your life who fall into these categories and label them NS, OU, PD, MD, NSEE, CB, or O (for any others who make you feel bad but don't quite fit the categories—you may even want to make up your own names for them).

1. _____   _____

2. _____   _____

3. _____   _____

4. _____   _____

5. _____   _____

You've identified the people who make you feel bad. Now, you need to make an important decision: should you completely eliminate them from your life (*not* Michael Corleone's "swimming with the fishes" style, of course), or should you no longer discuss your career with them? You may well find that family members and people you can't avoid fall into the latter category.

To help you through this process, both logically and emotionally, write your concerns about eliminating or partially excluding each of these people from your life in your journal.

It also helps to realize that many people have come in and out of your life through the years. Recognize that those people who have treated you badly never meant to hurt you. They had their own issues but came into your life to teach you a valuable lesson.

Perhaps as you prepare to move on from them, you may have some insight as to what you were supposed to learn from each one. Write a journal entry about each person starting off with:

I believe that _____ *came into my life so I would learn:*

These people have their own lessons to learn. By you allowing them to treat you badly, they aren't provided with the lesson they need to grow as people. It is not your responsibly to teach them these lessons, but through your disassociation with them, they may discover these truths on their own.

You must decide how to let them go. You can confront them and end the relationship, send them a letter, or simply drift apart.

Finally, for each person you want to move on from, choose someone you want to embrace more deeply into your life. This helps you get through your loss of one relationship by replacing it with another. Now, you'll focus on the time you spend with someone who enriches your life rather than with the negative person. You deserve to be surrounded by supportive, encouraging, loving people as you pursue your career dream.

Ending personal relationships can be extremely stressful. This chapter may not be enough for you to take action. If this is the case, seek advice from people you trust, or talk to a professional about how to move forward.

week 29
ANCHORMAN

I n the 1970s, Veronica Corningstone struts feminism right
into top-rated anchorman Ron Burgundy's macho newsroom.
She's ambitious and determined and won't let puff stories like
cat fashion shows keep her down. Veronica doesn't care about the
limited thinking of her coworkers. She has a dream, and she is
going to make it happen.

Veronica was well aware that there weren't any female anchors,
but in a world that kept telling her no, she didn't stop until she got
her shot. And when she did, she was ready for it.

As you learned from Week 28, for every dream there are people who have a plethora of reasons why your dream won't come
true. After hearing enough nos, you might start to buy into them.
Those reasons become your excuses so you don't have to try other
ways to find a yes.

This week, I'm going to have you look at other people's reasons
that have become your excuses. They are those you've made to
yourself so many times that they've turned into your own limiting
beliefs. You remember from Week 23, those general statements
that you've turned into facts, such as:

+ If I haven't made it by age __ I never will.
+ They don't like to hire women to do that job.
+ You have to be related to someone in Hollywood to make it.
+ It's hard for someone of my race to be given a break doing __.

What I find so interesting is how some people can pass off their limiting beliefs as facts and share them with others.

I'm not claiming there aren't obstacles regarding age, gender, race, religion, etc. There are. However, if there is anyone with whom you share one or more of these characteristics who's doing what you want to do, then you can do it, too! And if there isn't anyone to inspire you in this way, then you, like Veronica Corningston, must be a trailblazer. Being determined to make it, what other option do you have but to focus on how you can succeed instead of why you can't?

There are limiting beliefs for *everyone*. I'll use age as an example.

I have clients over fifty who tell me they can't get work because they're *too old*. People only want to hire the young, new "It Guy."

I also have clients under thirty-five who tell me that they can't work because they're *too young*.

People only want to hire the older, more experienced guy.

Finally, I have clients between the ages of thirty-five and fifty who tell me they can't work because they're *stuck in the age gap*: not young enough to be the young, new "It Guy" and not old enough to be the older, more experienced guy.

See? There's an excuse for everyone.

Let's examine any limiting beliefs you may have as to how the industry is hindering your career. These are the beliefs you feel to the core of your soul and that act as inhibitors for your advancement. These may be some of them: you aren't related to anyone, you don't have enough money, you're not the right gender, race, religion, age, etc. You may even have proof and resent that I'm suggesting they could perhaps be beliefs and not facts.

Write all of your limiting beliefs that are stopping you from moving forward in your career.

1. _____

2. _____

3. _____

4. _____

5. _____

What if these weren't true? What if a teenager from the same circumstances as you shares your dream and has a fierce desire to pursue it? This young person asks if it's possible. Deep down you know when it comes to working in this industry almost anything's possible. In your heart, you know you can't bring yourself to destroy this teen's dream.

Imagine that all the limiting beliefs you wrote above are those of the teenager. Write two empowering beliefs to counter each of the limiting ones.

For example:

Limiting belief: Producers don't want to give female cinematographers a break.
Empowering beliefs:
1. There are women DPs, and if they can do it, I can do it.
2. My artistic talent and interviewing skills will transcend gender.

Limiting belief 1:_____

_____

Empowering beliefs:

1. _____

_____

2. _____

_____

Limiting belief 2:_____

_____

Empowering beliefs:

1. _____

_____

2. _____

_____

Limiting belief 3:_____

_____

Empowering beliefs:

1. _____

_____

2. _____

_____

Limiting belief 4:_____

_____

Empowering beliefs:

1. _____

_____

2. _____

_____

Limiting belief 5:_____

_____

Empowering beliefs:

1. _____

_____

2. _____

_____

Here's a summarizing thought—when you first decided you were going to pursue your dream, you didn't begin with a list of reasons why you couldn't make it. Isn't that right? So why would you get sucked into the trap of listening to other people's reasons for you not to succeed?

Focus on Empowering Beliefs!

In your journal, write a paragraph on each new belief describing how it will enhance the quality of your life, starting with: *I believe...*

MR. HOLLAND'S OPUS

lenn Holland takes a teaching job to pay the bills as he works toward his goal of composing his opus. As the years go by, through tragedy and triumph, he touches the lives of his family and students with passionate music.

Wouldn't it be useful to have a tool that can instantly propel you into the emotional state of your choice? That tool is called an anchor. Anchoring is the process of creating a neurological association by applying a specific stimulus to one or more of the five senses while you are in a heightened emotional state. These are five types of anchors:

+ Kinesthetic (feeling/touch)
+ Auditory (hearing)
+ Visual (seeing)
+ Olfactory (smelling—the strongest anchor because it goes straight to the brain)
+ Gustatory (tasting)

Music is a very powerful anchor for most people. For instance, upon hearing the song "White Christmas," it may remind you of a specific person in your family who would sing that song at every family get-together. Or maybe you simply make an association between holiday music and the emotional state of holiday time. This may fill you with good spirits, or quite possibly the opposite, depending on your stress level during the holidays.

There are certain songs that remind you of your youth, your prom, camp, or a movie you loved. Certain types of music can uplift you while other types of music can fuel your frustration while sitting in traffic.

In this chapter, I'm going to teach you how to create emotional anchors using music. They will help you access the emotions you desire in the time it takes to listen to a song.

We will be focusing on the auditory anchor because you will be listening to a song that makes you feel a certain way.

First, decide, what are some of the resourceful states you want to be able to access. Choose emotional states that you would want for an interview, audition, meeting, on the job, etc. The following are some emotional states you may want to consider:

+ Excitement
+ Power
+ Unstoppable
+ Pride

- Gratitude
- Confidence
- Love

Three emotional states you would like to be able to anchor are:

1. _____

2. _____

3. _____

Second, choose a song that makes you feel that emotion when you listen to it. For example, when I want to feel motivated, I listen to "Eye of the Tiger." If I want to feel love, I listen to James Taylor's "Something in the Way She Moves." Listening to Incubus' "Drive" makes me feel powerful in my career.

Once you have a song that already gets you in touch with the desired emotion, there are three ways to deeply set the anchor.

The first and best way is to already be in the emotional state. While in that natural state of the emotion, you set your anchor. This is the most challenging way because you need to have the song with you when you're in the peak state of the emotion. Carry an iPod with you or keep the CDs in your car. When something happens that makes you feel that emotion, listen to your song. Having selected a song anchoring you to empowerment, once you get a call for work that makes you feel this way, put on your song and play it loudly. Fully experience the emotions and the music!

An example of this happening in a natural state is at a wedding when the couple dances to their song. They are in such a heightened state of love and happiness that for years to come when they hear that song these emotions will surge within them.

The second is to use sense memory. Sense memory is a technique in which you focus on a memory where you felt your desired emotion. Let's use excitement as the emotion you want to anchor. You will close your eyes, relax your body, and imagine yourself in that moment when you felt totally excited. Using all of your senses, recall exactly how you felt in that memory when you were feeling excitement. What do you see; who's with you; what are the sounds, smells, tastes associated with your memory? When you are at the peak state of feeling that excitement, play your song.

You can do this multiple times with different memories of excitement, stacking the memories and deeply anchoring your excited state to the song.

The third is to use your imagination to get you to your peak emotional state. This technique is just like the second way only, instead of using a real memory, you're imagining a situation in which you would feel the desired emotion. For example, you want to feel excitement and pride. Receiving an award for your work would make you feel that way. Create a detailed image of winning the award. You will close your eyes, imagine what the award is, who else is nominated, and who's at your table. Imagine who the presenter is and hear your name called. Hear the thunderous applause, the glowing accolades, and the band's crescendo as you make your way to the stage. What are the scents in the room? Hear yourself saying your acceptance speech. Whom are you thanking? For what are you grateful? Let your body fully feel the feelings of accepting that award. As tears of joy are rolling down your face, play your song.

You can do this multiple times with different images of excitement and pride. Stack the feelings and deeply anchor your excited, proud state to the song.

The key to a successful anchor is that it thrusts you to the peak of the emotion—give it 100 percent!

1. Write an event in the future where you would like to be in control of your emotional state.

_____

2. Choose a song to anchor to that state.

_____

3. All week, use the above techniques to bring yourself to the peak of your desired emotional state. Then play your song, stacking your emotional anchor. When the time is right, play your song and enjoy the power of a music anchor!

FLASHDANCE

A lex Owens is a woman with a dream of being a ballerina. If she gets accepted to ballet school, it will be very costly, so Alex works two jobs as a welder and as an exotic dancer. She saves money and keeps in touch with what she loves to do: dance.

Alex understood the nature of the dance industry. Like the entertainment industry, it can be an unstable, emotional, financial rollercoaster. Having a clear perspective of the nature of the industry is crucial if you plan to be in it for the long haul. You could classify the nature of this industry as unstable, unpredictable, slow, freelance, etc. And as in any industry, along with the drawbacks there are benefits.

Let's start with writing what you love about the industry:

1. _____

2. _____

3. _____

4. _____

5. _____

6. _____

7. _____

8. _____

Look at how our industry differs from the following jobs by factoring in the benefits and drawbacks of each profession:

Teaching

    Benefits: tenure, health benefits, set hours, time off for summer, making a difference

    Drawbacks: standardized methods make it monotonous, low to average pay, difficult students and, occasionally, difficult parents

Farming

    Benefits: work at home, usually with your family, contributing to the world's food needs

    Drawbacks: hard on your body, weather can ruin your crop, insects, bad growth, change in market costs

Investment banking

    Benefits: Big money, extravagant lifestyle, lots of perks

    Drawbacks: long hours, no time to enjoy your money or perks, high stress level with possible health risks

Working in retail

    Benefits: Steady hours, employee discount, easy to get coverage for days off, start at low wages but room to grow or to earn commissions

Drawbacks: Stores go out of business, same place/same job every day, have to deal with nasty customers who are always right

Evaluate what you consider to be the benefits and drawbacks of our industry. These are some examples:

Benefits: you get to be creative, there's potential for a big payday, variety, you can be famous, and you're not working 9-5

Drawbacks: you don't have a steady paycheck and health benefits, you can be hot one year and not the next, loss of privacy and long periods without work

Note: If you're new to the industry and are not sure what the benefits and drawbacks are, ask experienced people on your Contact List or ask your mentors.

Benefits	Drawbacks
_____	_____
_____	_____
_____	_____
_____	_____
_____	_____
_____	_____

Whether you want to be in this industry for the long or the short haul, it's important you recognize the benefits and drawbacks. As a result, you can *be prepared for both*.

Financial stability is one of the areas that must command your attention. The industry is ever changing. Some clients tell me that a long time ago there was enough union work to go around. Today, there are, in most cases, fewer union jobs than union members. It is important to plan financially for this climate. That means having supplemental, parallel, or passive income coming in. It is perfectly acceptable to have a job other than your chosen craft. Some people choose to have their "other job" be within the industry, so they can continue to create new relationships.

Emotional stability is equally important. When you know how talented you are and how hard you're willing to work, it's very frustrating to see others doing what you want to do and taking it for granted. Having an unfulfilled dream is emotionally difficult. Another difficult emotional aspect of our industry is what my friend Diane, a very successful actress, writer, and author, calls "The-day-after-Christmas Blues." She's referring to the feeling that occurs after completing a great job. To do what you love on a project with people you've grown attached to and then have it end can be traumatic.

It's also vital to have alternative creative outlets. Sometimes when you're not working, the unrecognized root of frustration and unhappiness is stemming from your lack of expression of creativity. For a creative person, relying on work alone to satisfy you creatively can be a big mistake.

Research and create a starting plan for maintaining stability in our unstable industry.

1. Financial Stability: Speak to a financial planner or someone you know who has financial success in our industry from additional sources of income. When you are working, even if it seems as if it will last forever, save for your future. Research the patterns of our industry's past to learn from them. Change can happen. The rug can be pulled out from under an entire media at anytime. Be smart, be prepared.

2. Emotional Stability: Have someone to talk to with whom you can work through your emotions. Be sure there is balance in your life. When your career isn't on a high, you'll have other interests and people fulfilling you.

3. Creative Stability: Find other ways to express and fulfill your creative needs.

week 32
ROCK STAR

After lead singer Chris Cole is kicked out of a Steel Dragon tribute band, he gets the opportunity of a lifetime. He is hired as the lead singer of the band he idolizes. Overnight, he goes from rock fan to rock legend. But after hard living on the road, losing his girlfriend, and not being taken seriously as a songwriter, Chris discovers that he's lost his own identity.

Chris was the prime example of the fake-it-'til-you-make-it attitude. He lived and breathed Steel Dragon until he became their lead singer. If you want to be an A-lister, you may want to learn a few lessons from Chris about fakin' it 'til you make it. I'm not suggesting that you lie about what you've done. Instead, it's the attitude of perseverance that you want to emulate.

Do you believe based solely on your talent and passion for what you do that you should be noticed and hired? This belief is a *major* misconception in the entertainment industry. It's too chancy to trust that people will find your work as exceptional as you do. They aren't buying a product; they are buying a perception (that's why stars have publicists).

To help you "own" your attitude of perseverance in an industry

177

based on perception, you will work on creating a personal brand. Who are you, and what makes you unique in this industry?

My version of creating a personal brand is to design a statement that sums you up—one that you will "live up to." For example, Michael Jordan is branded the best basketball player of all times. He wasn't at first. But he probably believed he would be, and then lived up to that belief.

An exercise to help you get started is to choose three people you admire in the industry. You don't need to know them. Imagine you're interviewing them on the following topics. Write in your journal what you believe they would say about the following topics:

1. Their image/appearance
2. Their professional strengths
3. What it is they value
4. Their personal brand

In your journal, write one trait you would like to share with each person.

By creating your brand, you create the perception of yourself that you want people to see. It will influence your marketing materials, your way of dressing, and your way of being.

Again in your journal:

1. What are your professional strengths and attributes?
2. What is your leading professional attribute?

3. What makes you different from your competition?

4. What do you value?

5. What special interests do you have?

6. What personality traits make you unique?

7. What do people hiring you expect from you?

8. How would you like to be perceived?

9. How are you perceived?

The last two questions are interesting ones since how you would "like" to be perceived isn't always how you *are* perceived. It's important to consult industry professionals to ask them how they perceive you and to see if your opinion is correct.

When I first pursued acting and people asked me what roles I was right for, I'd say, "I'm the girl next door," because I love romantic comedies.

The response was, "No, you're not. You're the girl who lives down the street and steals the girl next door's boyfriend." Shocked, I said that I would never do that! No one was saying that I would. They were saying that at face value with my looks, figure, and attitude, I was not the stereotypical girl next door.

Some people "look the part." If you want to fight what people see, you'd better be determined and certain that you can change what they see.

How important is it to look the part? I know a DP who wears fake glasses. Many others joke about changing their last names to something that sounds foreign. If people don't know you, sometimes creating a perception to meet their expectations can work to your advantage. Other times, creating a breakout style for yourself is the right way to go.

Ask yourself, "How can I make people who hire me perceive me differently from my competitors?" Be distinctive by creating a new category or putting a new spin on old terminology. An operator I know always said, "Top of the Howdy" when he called people. He became branded as "the top-of-the-howdy guy." Later, when HD had just started taking off, he decided he wanted to be known as "the industry HD expert." He immediately called publications, pitched himself as such, and they asked him to write articles. He then used the articles to market himself to others. Before long, he was training top directors and DPs on HD.

You can offer something no one else does. Back in the day, it was owning your own equipment. Now, perhaps it's pre-shooting your shots on video and making a DVD for the director/producer before they put it on film. You can create a unique thank-you gift. Or like one of the top still photographers did, invent your own way of delivering your product. In her case, she designed a program for identifying the photos. This gave the photo editors lots of extra information, to make their job easier.

Get creative and invent a new style, new buzz words, or new attributes that they can't live without.

For your classification, is there a need in the industry that is not being met?

Imagine how you would feel if your personal brand were:

"Wiley Coyote with a Panahead"

Or

"A Bon Vivant in a lab coat"

Or

"Perseverance, passion, and heart to beat the odds"

Each statement sets off different emotions in you. Your personal brand should trigger the emotions you want to feel and to have others feel when they're around you.

What is the primary feeling you want people to get when they think of your personal brand? _____

_____

What is the secondary feeling you want people to get when they think of your personal brand? _____

_____

You can't be all things to all people. Capitalize on your strengths. If that turns some people off, so be it. It's up to you to tell people how to feel about you. What problem do you solve? How can you make their lives easier?

Creating your personal brand is about recognizing your special talents, skills, and personal qualities then summarizing them in a statement. Look over everything you've learned in this chapter. Chisel it down to a single sentence that encompasses all a person needs to know to get the perception of the you you're trying to create.

This gives *you* a clear and exclusive identity. I emphasize you because your personal brand statement is not something you're going to share with people. This is not a logo or a statement for the homepage of your Web site. This is an exciting, empowering, creative statement, that when you say it to yourself, will put you in the mindset of success. Here are some examples:

+ A distinguished gentleman with plume in hand
+ An energizer bunny at the edit bay
+ Creative woman of action
+ Unbreakable conqueror
+ Strength, leadership, artistry
+ Mistress of re-invention
+ Imaginative architect of cinematic storytelling

Remember, Michael Jordan was not the greatest basketball player of all time when he started in the NBA, but I imagine he believed he would be. It was that belief that gave him the mindset and work ethic to actually become his brand.

Once you have your personal brand statement, use it as a "mantra" before an interview, meeting, or audition.

Brainstorm some ideas for your personal brand statement until you've got one that you love.

You may even choose to have different statements for different circumstances.

PAY IT FORWARD

Trevor McKinney, a young boy, is given an assignment by his social studies teacher. He must think of something to change the world and put the plan into action. Trevor's idea is to do three good deeds and to ask the recipients to "pay them forward" with more good deeds. The results of his actions spread good will to the lives of his mother, his teacher, and people from city to city, strangers he will never know.

You've spent the last thirty-two weeks focused on yourself. This week is different. It's about helping others to achieve their goals. You may be wondering what this has to do with your career. For the answer, I ask you to recall that in my introduction I wrote, "What you do in all aspects of your life affects your career as much as your career affects your life." The action of doing good deeds has the immediate effect of making both the recipient and giver feel great. Then your good spirits fill you with positive energy and you are a joy to be around. You can't deny how beneficial this attitude is to your career!

The most important part of this exercise is to do your good deeds unconditionally. Many times I've heard people complain about how they've helped someone and how that person hadn't reciprocated. When I asked if they helped with this expectation, they shifted uncomfortably and replied, "No." Remember, make a commitment to want nothing more than to make someone feel good.

List five people on your Contact List you would like to help this week.

1. _____
2. _____
3. _____
4. _____
5. _____

For each person, decide if you are going to help openly or anonymously. You may even take a page from the movie script and ask the person for whom you're doing the good deed to pay it forward.

The following are ideas for good deeds:

+ Make anonymous donations to a struggling artist/craft person
+ Offer to make an introduction to someone they should know
+ Hire them for a day thereby helping them to build their credits

- Offer to take care of their child if they have a meeting or audition
- Forward a job lead that they wouldn't have known about

Complete the following template so you will have documentation of your good deeds. You can refer to it when you're feeling blue. Remembering how good you made someone else feel can be a real mood booster.

1. Person to help: _____

Plan of action: _____

_____

_____

Person's reaction to your help: _____

_____

_____

2. Person to help: _____

Plan of action: _____

_____

_____

Person's reaction to your help: _____

_____

_____

3. Person to help: _____

Plan of action: _____

_____

_____

Person's reaction to your help: _____

_____

_____

4. Person to help: _____

Plan of action: _____

_____

_____

Person's reaction to your help: _____

_____

_____

5. Person to help: _____

Plan of action: _____

_____

_____

Person's reaction to your help: _____

_____

_____

If you are disappointed by the reaction of any of your people, don't fill out the template for that individual. Instead, pick another person for whom to do a good deed. While the objective is to help others unconditionally, my objective for you is to have a positive experience with it.

Should you come across an unappreciative recipient, don't take it personally. There are many people who struggle with accepting help.

The more you help people, the better you feel. Although sometimes they may even help you in return, you can feel even better knowing you did it unconditionally.

1. Schedule the time to help your five people.

2. Fill out the templates when your tasks are completed.

FIELD OF DREAMS

"If you build it, he will come." That's what the voice said; therefore, Ray Kinsella decides to build a baseball field in his cornfield. What does Ray expect to happen? Whom is he expecting? People think he is crazy, but he keeps working on his field until it is done!

Now that you're three quarters of the way through the book, it's time to look at what your expectations are regarding what you think "should" be happening. If forced to relinquish your expectations, you may feel disappointment. What's important is that you work through them to discover the possibilities that will unfold.

To expect is defined as:

1. to consider likely
2. to consider reasonable or due
3. to consider obligatory; require

The definitions accelerate in their intensity (likely, due, obligatory) as do our expectations as time passes.

What do you think "should" be happening? After all, you've

been learning the tools, the mindsets, and taking action. Have any of your expectations not been met?

Write an unfulfilled expectation that continues to frustrate you:

_____

_____

It's a competitive industry that can be tough on passionate, hardworking dreamers. You would do almost anything to know whether you're wasting your time or in for a payoff. Palm readers make a great deal of money off of artists. Did you expect that it would be hard to pursue a dream that has no guarantee of coming to fruition? Did you assume that with hard work and talent you were a shoo-in for success?

When you first committed to pursuing a career in the entertainment industry you had certain expectations. In regards to those expectations, answer the following questions:

1. How would you have defined success?

_____

_____

2. How long did you think it would take you to succeed?

_____

_____

3. With whom did you think you would be working?

_____

_____

4. What were your long-term goals?

_____

_____

5. What hours would you be working?

_____

_____

6. How would work integrate with your personal life?

_____

_____

7. What were other expectations?

_____

_____

8. Eight months ago, when you started reading this book, what were your expectations?

_____

_____

9. How have your expectations been met/surpassed?

_____

_____

10. Where have your expectations not been met?

_____

_____

You could look at your unmet expectations and grow bitter and frustrated. You could convince yourself that time is running out and put fear, doubt, and desperation into your future. But that won't help you. You don't get what you want, you get what you expect.

Review your expectations; cross out any that are negative. If you get what you expect, why would you want to expect anything negative?

To counter the frustration of expectations not met, acknowledge the growth and positive changes you've made in the last eight months.

When you feel good about who you are, you allow better people, experiences, jobs, and opportunities into your life.

If you find your thoughts trailing back to your old expectations, interrupt them by focusing on what's working.

and...Action!

1. How have you shown commitment to your goals?

_____

_____

_____

2. Where have you achieved balance? _____

_____

_____

3. How many new relationships have you created? _____

4. What character qualities have you acquired or improved?
(Example: patience, generosity, strategic thinking, focusing)

_____

_____

_____

5. How many people have you helped? _____

LAWS OF ATTRACTION

*T*he laws of attraction have nothing to do with this romantic comedy couple getting married. Divorce attorneys Audrey Woods and Daniel Rafferty owe that to a night of drinking. But being focused on each other's every move in the courtroom brings these opposites together.

This week's focus is on the laws of attraction, of which there's been much talk lately. It's basically the theory that "like attracts like." I find that people need to discover its power on their own to truly understand what a powerful tool it is to master.

The thoughts that you think attract more of what you think about. In other words, you get what you focus on. So, if you are focusing on lack of work, lack of money, or lack of help, the laws of attraction say that you will attract more of the same.

Consider this pattern as a self-fulfilling prophecy. You think negative thoughts about not working. In turn, this makes you feel bad, causing you to think more bad thoughts and the spiral continues downward. Then you have an opportunity present itself, like an interview for a job. If you think you can mask your desperate, negative feelings, you are most likely wrong. They seep out despite your efforts. You don't get the job, which makes you think more negative thoughts and so on.

Luckily, it works the opposite way as well. If you're thinking good thoughts, you'll feel good and attract good things because people will be attracted to you and your great outlook. If you choose your thoughts carefully, you can create your career the way a writer creates a script, through a series of scenes that build and build.

The beauty of this theory is you can create thoughts that will make you feel a certain way even if there isn't anything going on in your career to support them. During Week 30, you were taught a method for using your imagination to create the feelings of truthfully living through your imagined circumstances.

Your subconscious mind doesn't know if your imagined events are real or fake; it simply responds to the feelings your body is experiencing. That's why when you have an anxiety dream you can wake up in a sweat with your heart racing. Your subconscious mind doesn't know the difference.

In the following exercise, you're going to create your career's "coming attraction." You know when you watch a television show and they do that montage of what's coming up next week? You're going to create a montage for your career.

Start by brainstorming ten snippets of what you would like to attract in your career. (Examples: I see my name on my reserved spot on a studio lot, I'm walking down a red carpet, or I'm watching my credit scrolling at the end of a movie. They can also be material snippets like a specific car you could see yourself driving or in a house you would like to own.)

1. _____

2. _____

3. _____

4. _____

5. _____

6. _____

7. _____

8. _____

9. _____

10. _____

Write them as if you were arranging a montage scene. This order is your career's "coming attraction."

Montage: _____

_____

_____

_____

_____

_____

_____

_____

_____

_____

_____

_____

Memorize the order of these clips so you can visualize your "coming attraction" multiple times a day. The key to this exercise is to really feel the feelings of knowing that this is your future.

This is usually around the time when your cynical voice wants to chime in. It's probably saying, "Okay, so I create this visualization where I'm basically asking the universe for what I want. I believe that it's already mine with blind faith and then I wait to receive it? Yeah, right!"

I want you to remember that this is just one tool in this book. By no means am I suggesting that you stop being proactive and wait for the universe to drop opportunities in your lap. But what do you really have to lose by experimenting to see if the laws of attraction can really work for you?

When I was first introduced to the laws of attraction, I did my own experiment. I hadn't had an audition in over six months. I decided that for an entire month I would visualize getting an audition and do nothing else except let my new manager submit me. Three weeks into the experiment, a caller on my cell phone offered an audition that he claimed I'd submitted myself for. Knowing I hadn't put myself up for anything, I called my manager. She said it was a legitimate project in the breakdowns, but she had submitted me for a different role. I pointed out that even though she'd submitted me, he had called *my* cell phone, which wasn't listed on my resume because her number was. She called the director to get to the bottom of it and discovered that he'd picked me out of the Player's Directory. If you're not familiar with the Player's Directory, it is a book with thousands of actors from the biggest stars to complete unknowns. My manager even commented that in all of her years in the industry, she'd never heard of anyone getting a call from the directory.

Hmmmmm...pretty interesting. I'm a believer. If your voice is now saying, "Yes, well, that was a miracle." Maybe so, but why can't miracles happen to you, too?

Visualize your "coming attraction" at least once a day (more if possible) for the whole week.

week 36
SERENDIPITY

S trangers Jonathan and Sara meet over a struggle for the last pair of gloves while Christmas shopping for their significant others. There is something magical about the rest of the evening that they spend together. But Sara is unable to trust the magic and chooses to let fate decide if they are "meant to be." Tiny serendipities happen along the way, bringing them within seconds of each other. Finally a starry, snowy night reunites them, serendipity fulfilled!

In Week 34, you learned that you get what you expect, so it's important to expect good things. In Week 35, you learned about the laws of attraction and how you can attract what you want into your life. Now I'll have you look at the "magic" in your life. I like to believe that if you expect good things and do what you can to attract them into your life, then you will get some serendipitous help along the way.

Serendipity is defined as:

1. an aptitude for making desirable discoveries by accident
2. good fortune; luck

It's important to believe. You must hold onto the faith that your career is what you're meant to do and somehow, someway, you will make it. Without this belief, you have no hope. It is faith and hope that get you through the rough patches. But it must be unconditional faith—you can't put parameters or time lines on faith. You just have to take the leap.

To facilitate the leap of faith, it's important to build a case. I offer as evidence some personal examples of serendipity. I had been in Los Angeles for two years without any SAG work or understanding of the business. I decided to leave a bad roommate situation with a depressed, frustrated writer and found a new roommate, a jealous, resentful actress. Simultaneously, the restaurant where I was waiting tables went bankrupt, so I had no income. My sister was thinking about moving out to LA, but I would have to wait three months for her to graduate college. I was three thousand miles away from my home and everyone I loved. I knew I couldn't stay in the actress's apartment. I felt hopeless thinking my only option was to go home...until something serendipitous happened. I went out with the actress and a friend of hers. The friend asked me how the living arrangement was going. I told her that it would be best if I could find other arrangements for the next three months. The girl said, "I can't believe this! My father is a professor at UCLA. He is taking a three-month sabbatical overseas and can't bring his dog. The dog sitter just fell through." The next thing I knew, I was living in a high-rise on the Wilshire corridor with a doorman and valet, rent-free with

Bernie, the Bernese mountain dog. This twist of fate gave me the confidence to continue following my dreams. Four months later, I was in development on my first pilot and living with my sister and our new puppy, Jake.

I had a client, an aerial news photographer, who wanted to do feature film aerial photography. Neither of us knew anyone in that profession. I taught him the basics on how to research what steps needed to be taken. The more we talked, the more disheartened he became, realizing how small the niche was in this field. He asked about working in commercials, instead. I went onto the Web to show him a list of commercial companies to research, but discovered that I couldn't find the desired Web site. I was forced to do a Google search. The very first site that came up was "The 411." Now, "The 411" has hundreds of company listings and lots of banner advertisements. But this particular day at this particular time, the advertising banner that popped up was for an aerial photography company. We both got chills. His spirit got a huge lift at the realization that "something" was helping him and was on his side as he pursued his dreams.

The production of my television show, *Prescriptions*, quickly became known as the "charmed production." Anything we needed just seemed to fall into our lap. When we needed a location, one of my producers would bump into an old friend who just happened to have our exact location. When we needed a cool guest star, someone's schedule would serendipitously open up. The whole cast and crew was aware of how charmed we were, elevating the spirit to a new level. This was the most fun-filled production I've ever worked on.

When you get frustrated and begin to lose faith, it's events like these that can be a reminder that you're on the right path. Because you get what you expect and you attract what you need, it's always important to look for these magical signs.

What were the serendipitous or miraculous events from your life? This week, write in your journal as many signs, moments, and events that have occurred in your life.

Any time you find yourself questioning whether you're on the right path, turn to these pages in your journal for a boost of faith and continue with your leap!

LIFE IS BEAUTIFUL

A Jewish waiter, Guido, falls in love with Dora, a schoolteacher, from a nearby city. They enjoy a fairy-tale courtship, marry, and have a son. They live happily together until German forces occupy Italy during World War II. Guido's family is taken to a concentration camp. It is there that he finds a way to communicate with his wife. To keep his son from being fearful, he pretends the whole experience is a game.

When you look back at what people have lived through in our history, and what many still live with today (wars, slavery, famine), you realize how lucky you are.

Gratitude is a powerful tool to master. Focusing on what you do have, acknowledging whom you love and who loves you, fills you with happiness. It's about recognizing what you have right now and being grateful for all of it. Appreciating the small things that bring you joy on a daily basis will keep you emotionally intact when things in your career are not going as you'd hoped. This attitude of gratitude can help keep you going until things turn around.

Even in the devastation of a concentration camp, Guido was grateful to be with his son and to have contact with his wife. Living for them was his reason to live. What are your reasons to live? For what are you grateful?

As you spend the week examining gratitude, create a list that you can re-read whenever you feel down. It's important to write your list before this feeling takes over. Sometimes it's hard to acknowledge what you're grateful for when you're feeling bad. Take the time this week to fill in your gratitude list.

GRATITUDE LIST

I am grateful for:

1. _____

2. _____

3. _____

4. _____

5. _____

6. _____

7. _____

8. _____

9. _____

10. _____

One of the easiest ways to develop an attitude of gratitude is to have an object that will remind you to feel grateful. Choose something:

a picture, a rock or shell, or a nostalgic token. Either put it in a spot where you will see it multiple times a day or carry it with you.

Every time you touch or see that object, remind yourself of one or more things for which you are truly grateful.

Another way is to recognize the everyday things that bring you joy. For me, it's snuggling with my two giant dogs, writing, acting, taking "me time" (that can be reading a chick lit book or soaking in a lavender bubble bath), calling my family, and eating one of my fiancé's delicious gourmet meals. I also "take time to smell the roses," literally.

What brings you everyday joy?

1. _____
2. _____
3. _____
4. _____
5. _____

It is easy to focus on what you don't have and what's not going your way. Instead, challenge yourself to focus on what you *do* have and what *can* come your way. The results will be worth it!

Read your gratitude list at least once a day.

week ***38***

GANDHI

This biopic movie describes the life of Mahatma Gandhi, a political leader in India, who frees his country from British rule through peaceful means. His spiritual philosophy of non-violent protest gives hope and inspiration to people all over the world for generations to come.

In Week 33, you got a taste of doing good deeds for others. This week is about doing *good* on a larger scale.

Most people spend their time focusing on their own circumstances and those of their immediate circle. And when the circumstances related to your career are not going well, complaining about it becomes an easy route to take. In this downward slide, you start comparing yourself to others who are finding more success, which makes you envious and resentful. You find going to your supplemental job makes you bitter and frustrated.

Perhaps, when you're feeling this way, a little perspective is in order. With all your ups and downs, your constant is that you know what you're passionate about, and you have the courage to pursue those dreams. There are so many people who have dreams without the means or courage to pursue them. Others, never in their lifetime find something to be passionate about. Still there are those who may have dreams and passions but, due to life's circumstances such as illness, poverty, handicaps, abuse, and tragedy, will never be able to pursue them. The latter are the people you will focus on this week. They need and are deserving of your contribution.

Here, then, in a nutshell, is the perspective:

Compared to people suffering with life-altering situations, your career not happening in the time frame that you expect really isn't as tragic as it feels. As an additional affirmation, this is a good time to re-read your gratitude list from last week.

This is the point at which someone (who only focuses on his own problem) argues with me that while he acknowledges his life isn't as bad as someone with a terminal illness, this is his life and he has his own problems.

In answer to that I say, "Then it's time you made the problems of others your problems." In taking on the subject matter of this week, you will grow in three ways:

- You will be helping others who are in need.
- You will be constantly reminded to keep perspective on how fortunate you are.
- In the spirit of this book, you will be creating relationships that will benefit your career.

Have I piqued your interest? This week's "And…Action" has you giving back. My request is that, whenever possible, you be directly involved. By all means contribute financially if you can afford it, but the true spirit of this assignment is to get involved. The more you reach out to others, the more you are touched by them and their circumstances. That's how you grow in the first two ways.

Growing in the third way is where strategy comes in. I had a friend in high school whose mother told her, "Honey, it's just as easy to fall in love with a rich guy as it is to fall in love with a poor one. So go out there and find yourself a rich one." As superficial as sending this message to a young girl sounds, the mother's intention was to show her daughter that the motive was the same—to genuinely fall in love. She wanted her daughter to recognize that she had the power to choose.

There are many worthwhile, charitable causes and many ways to choose which ones to become involved with. Why not select one that is not only close to your heart but also close to the heart of other industry people? The motive is the same—to help people. To maximize your time, you can offer help while creating relationships with people who have likeminded sensibilities.

A great example is Hollywood Heart, a nonprofit organization that sends children whose lives are affected by HIV to summer camp. They also have a filmmaking program for inner-city kids who would otherwise never have opportunities to learn about making movies. Many, if not most of the volunteers are in the industry and offer their time and talents to the program. These are people who have both a love for their industry and compassionate hearts. They sound like good people to know, don't they?

If you live in Los Angeles, finding a charitable organization with compassionate industry people is easy to do. You can find them at well known organizations such as Project Angel Food or Make-A-Wish Foundation. Smaller organizations that may fall under a parent charity can be harder to find, like From the Heart (a literacy organization). The parent charity is One Voice at www.firstbook.org. For information about From the Heart contact Chair Barri Evins at 310-657-7733. There are a multitude of others. All it takes is some research on your part.

Most research can be done online. Another way to find a good fit is to decide what's important to you and to ask the people on your Contact List if they're aware of any charities that match.

What causes are important to you? Whose life circumstances do you want to improve?

1. Go online to find five charitable organizations that touch your heart.

    1. _____

    2. _____

3. _____

4. _____

5. _____

2. Look at their calendar for the year and plan to attend at least one hands-on event for each over the course of the year to help you choose which one is right for you. Evaluate where your contribution is fulfilling as well as where you're being exposed to the people whose lives are being helped because of you.

Note: If you don't live in a major city but do have an entertainment community where you are, this week, start laying the foundation to start your own charitable organization. You could even look into creating a branch of a Hollywood charitable organization.

SCROOGED

*F*rank Cross, a cynical and selfish television executive, is haunted by the ghosts of Christmas past, present, and future before he realizes that he must change the way he treats people. Extreme cases call for extreme measures, and Frank is extremely self-absorbed, heartless, and mean to his employees.

Frank's "ghosts" were warning signs. Would you recognize the warning signs if you were overloading yourself with to-dos and pressure?

This week, I want you to evaluate how much you've put on your plate. Since there is so much stress and pressure in our industry, it's important for you to recognize warning signs.

They can range from the not-so-serious, such as forgetting where you put your keys, ignoring a few meals, and minor tasks slipping through the cracks, to the increasingly serious ones. These may include among others: addiction, burnout, hair loss, illness, forgetfulness, insomnia, muscle tension, and important tasks slipping through the cracks.

Imagine that at this moment you are visited by a ghost who says to you, "Look at your life! If you keep going like this you're in for trouble!" To what three things might that ghost be referring?

1. _____
2. _____
3. _____

Shortly after, another ghost appears and points out to the first one that *Eyes Wide Shut* wasn't shot in a day. It then turns to you and asks, "How did you get to the point where you are today?" What three things come to mind? What patterns, habits, or choices created your stress or pressure?

1. _____
2. _____
3. _____

A third ghost enters the picture: the ghost of the future. It says, "Perhaps you have looked at your past and perhaps you are clear about where you are, right now. But at this instant, are you willing to do what it takes to change?" If you keep ignoring the warning signs and continue on this path, what are the three things that you fear the future will have in store for you?

1. _____

2. _____

3. _____

To get through the day, do you rely on bad habits such as the regular intake of fast food? Do you neglect stress relievers like working out and meditation? Some say it takes twenty-one days to create a habit. But how long does it take to undo a habit? Change can happen in an instant. It's the decision to commit to making a change that can take a long time. Giving up certain bad habits, like drinking too much caffeine, can have annoying side affects like headaches, lethargy, and moodiness, causing you not to want to make the change. Others, such as creating a good habit of exercise, can quickly become addictive because of the release of endorphins and the release of stress.

Based on the three warning signs that the first ghost pointed out, what is one detrimental habit to your well-being that you would like to change right now?

_____

In your journal, write about the benefits of changing this habit. Once you really know why you want to change, how do you do it? As I stated above, first you must make the commitment to change. Then, figure out what your obstacles will be so you can determine how to overcome them. Let's say your bad habit is to ignore stress relievers such as meditation and exercise, and you want to install in its place the good habit of going to the gym. Your obstacles may be lack of motivation, lack of time, or lack of knowledge of what to do in a gym.

Obstacles for changing my bad habit into a good habit:

1. _____

2. _____

3. _____

Next, find ways to overcome the obstacles (you may need to seek advice for this part). For our first example above, to overcome lack of motivation, create a workout goal. Build in a reward for accomplishing it or join the gym with a friend and meet there. Having a partner gives you both motivation and accountability. It also solves obstacle number two; time you spend with friends can now be spent together in the gym. Start with a shorter workout, or join a gym very close to your home or office. The third obstacle is simple to overcome: ask a personal trainer to give you an orientation. You can go online to find workout advice (check out www.purestrength. com) or take a body sculpting class that's instructional.

Make it doable for yourself by breaking it down into manageable steps.

Heed the warnings of the ghosts and, like Scrooge, make a change in your life. What is one change you can commit to right now that will decrease the pressure you put on yourself?

_____

_____

_____

_____

PULP FICTION

Mistakes happen, guns go off, and people like Jules and Vincent find themselves in a bloody car with a dead body. Not being equipped to take care of their messy situation, they know they have to get someone in there to clean it up. They call on "the cleaner," Winston "The Wolf" Wolfe. Winston is the kind of guy who asks where you are and replies, "That's thirty minutes away. I'll be there in ten." He knows how to get things done.

Life can get messy sometimes, or to be more specific, your desk, closets, car, relationships, unfinished projects, and commitments can get messy. If you don't clean them up, they can consciously and unconsciously affect your career.

It's really amazing how much time you can spend thinking about how much you can't get done because you've got too much to do. Feeling overwhelmed is both mentally and physically draining. You end up giving enormous amounts of energy to things that have to get done but which aren't necessarily a priority.

The solution is time management. This week you are going to clean up your physical and mental drains.

Start by making a list of anything and everything that can be draining you emotionally: goals and expectations not achieved, unfinished projects, challenges you have encountered, people you are out of communication with, or any regrets you have.

LETTER

1. _____ _____

2. _____ _____

3. _____ _____

4. _____ _____

5. _____ _____

6. _____ _____

7. _____ _____

8. _____ _____

9. _____ _____

10. _____ _____

Make a list of an incomplete personal business: anything that needs to be fixed, cleaned, or improved in your home, office, or car; health issues like doctor appointments that need to be made; investments or financial improvements that you're putting off.

LETTER

1. _____ _____
2. _____ _____
3. _____ _____
4. _____ _____
5. _____ _____
6. _____ _____
7. _____ _____
8. _____ _____
9. _____ _____
10. _____ _____

Now evaluate each of your drains by putting a letter in the letter column. "O" will mean it's an ongoing project that you will put time and energy into when necessary. "S" means you must set a date or time line to complete the task so it is over and done with. "C" means that you are complete with the situation and at this moment in time, have no intention of taking any action to change it.

Anything that is not an "O" or "S" is a "C." I know it can be hard to let go and to choose closure when it comes to friendships that have faded, burned bridges, or dead projects, but they are not serving you; they are simply taking up space and energy that can be better used.

After evaluating your drains, it's time to replenish your energy by eliminating either the drain itself or its cause.

The first step toward eliminating the things that consume, exhaust, and deplete your energy physically and emotionally is to recognize what they are.

Follow the four steps and use the template on the next page for each of your "S" drains and any of the "O" drains for which you have a step that can be taken toward their completion.

1. Schedule a time to handle each drain. Be sure to space out the times so you can manage everything.
2. Get support for those things that you would rather avoid.
3. Break the tasks into small, manageable steps and do them.
4. Build in a reward to motivate you through the process.

REPLENISH YOUR ENERGY TEMPLATE

Energy Drain:

_____

_____

I plan to handle this on _____/_____/_____

The person/people I can call to support me with this project is/are:

1. _____

2. _____

3. _____

Manageable tasks to complete this would be:

1. _____

2. _____

3. _____

4. _____

5. _____

My completion reward will be:

_____

_____

and...*Action!*

Put each of the tasks you've scheduled into your datebook, and forget about them until their date. Just knowing that they are scheduled to get done is a relief, even if the scheduled date is six months away.

SHAKESPEARE IN LOVE

iola is a wealthy young woman promised in marriage. Yet, she constantly dreams of becoming an actress. Her problem, besides her pending wedding, is that women are not allowed to be on the stage. Only men can be actors; they dress up and play the women's roles. Viola, her passion for her art so great, decides to risk everything and to sacrifice her identity to become an actress. By dressing up as a boy, Viola lands the leading role of Romeo in Will Shakespeare's play "Romeo and Juliet" and ultimately falls in love with the playwright.

You hear about it all the time, people making financial, family, and/or health sacrifices for their craft. Some may leave their home state or country. Others tolerate abusive behavior from superiors.

You've heard about the sacrifices, but have you thought about what they mean to you? What are you are willing to give up? What boundaries won't you cross? Please keep in mind that you may never need to make any sacrifices, but it's important to educate yourself should the situation present itself.

For example, I know many people in our industry who, at one point in their career, lived in their car. They sacrificed everything they had except the clothes on their backs and the cars that transported and housed them. If asked, they would say that they did it for their art and had no choice. They were determined to make a living only from their craft. It was this commitment that gave them the determination to succeed.

Now, while it makes for a great story on *Jimmy Kimmel Live!*, living in a car is not a sacrifice I've ever been willing to make. Perhaps my career would have gone in a different direction had I been living in a car, but I'm content with the choices I've made. Therefore, I've chosen to have other sources of income. However, I was never willing to allow them to interfere with my career. I always had jobs that gave me the flexibility to come and go for career-related opportunities.

FINANCIAL MUST-HAVES OR SACRIFICES

How much money do you need to earn per year? $_____

What are your parameters for an acceptable means of income? (Examples: What kinds of jobs will you take? How flexible must they be? For whom won't you work?)

_____

_____

_____

_____

_____

_____

Must you own a house? YES / NO

Must you drive a nice car? YES / NO

Must you wear expensive clothes and/or accessories? YES / NO

FAMILY MUST-HAVES OR SACRIFICES

Must you get married? YES / NO

Must you have children? YES / NO

If you have a family, are you willing to take jobs that require you to be away for long periods of time? YES / NO

Would you be willing to miss holidays or family milestones like birthdays, anniversaries, graduations, or sports games for your career? YES / NO

LIFE MUST-HAVES OR SACRIFICES

Must you work with people whom you like and respect? YES / NO

Must you work with people who speak nicely to you and who treat you with respect? YES / NO

If you live in a city without an entertainment industry community, would you be willing to move? YES / NO

Would you tolerate dangerous stress levels? YES/ NO

Would you work dangerously long hours? YES/ NO

Would you work in a truly hazardous situation? YES/ NO

There are also moral and ethical issues to ponder. I won't write about the unethical, immoral things I've heard people do to get a job. I'll just say, "Just because you can, doesn't mean you should."

Remember, a short-term fix could end up hurting you, and ultimately the industry, in the long run.

Consider your answers in this chapter. Seek advice on any issues
that concern or confuse you. There's no need to focus on them,
simply educate yourself about all aspects of this industry.

week 42
THE MUSE

*S*teven Phillips, a neurotic screenwriter with writer's block, needs major help to recover his edge. He turns to Sarah, who claims to be Zeus' daughter, a mythical Goddess. Steven will do and pay anything to keep his muse happy, especially as he discovers she is filled with blockbuster ideas.

Boy! After all the chapters on business (and after last chapter's look at the many sacrifices you have to consider), you are probably in need of a creative boost. Let's put you back in touch with what you love to do!

What do you do when you have a "creative block"? Whatever your area in the entertainment industry, this week, you will "find your muse."

A fun and stimulating way to accomplish this is through using any one of your five senses and possibly even a sixth sense—but that's another movie.

Try all the exercises or just the ones that appeal to your "sense" of choice.

Let's start with visual. There are many things to look at or watch when you need to find your muse, especially if your craft is a visual one like cinematography, production design, costume, or hair and makeup.

What are three things you can look at to discover what your muse has to offer? (Examples: watch a movie, go to a museum, or look through a photographic coffee table book.)

1. _____

2. _____

3. _____

Every time I have a writer's block, I pop in a romantic comedy DVD and enjoy. While I watch, I trust that my subconscious is working to solve my block. Without fail, before the end of the movie, I've solved my problem and I'm back at my computer.

What you hear can inspire your muse. It could include the sound of the waves at the ocean, songs that tell a story and express an emotion, or the sounds of a country night filled with crickets and frogs.

When I write, I tell my fiancé I'm going to the "beach house." I visualize the beach house and the view as I sit with my laptop. Then, I turn on my sound machine to hear the crashing of the ocean waves and let my muse fill my mind with ideas.

What might you listen to that could harmonize with your muse?

1. _____
2. _____
3. _____

For the sense of touch, I always turn to water for inspiration. I have discovered interesting character quirks under the spray of a hot shower, I've had plot breakthroughs in a bath, and many a script idea has presented itself to me in a steaming Jacuzzi.

What could you touch to make your muse feel like sharing some inspiration? (Examples: textured fabric, your favorite blanket, or cold steel.)

1. _____
2. _____
3. _____

If I really need some inspiration, I take my muse on an outing to my favorite movie theater at The Grove. My muse is no cheap date, though. In addition to a good visual movie, I must treat my muse's taste buds to her favorite flavor: root beer. Add to that some hot, buttered popcorn, and she's as happy as can be. By the time the movie is over, my muse has stories to tell or characters to invent.

What foods might the characters in your project eat? What might a meatball and spaghetti dinner inspire in an actor playing an Italian mobster or an ice cream cone inspire in a set decorator?

What three foods or flavors would tempt your muse?

1. _____

2. _____

3. _____

In Week 30, I told you that smell is the most powerful of the senses because it goes straight to your brain. Not only does my muse enjoy the taste of hot, buttered popcorn, but the smell of it can take me back to a Yonkers, New York movie theater. As a young girl, my dad took me to that theater to see *Star Wars* eleven times.

Experiment with scents. Maybe your muse would enjoy smoky musk, pine needles, hot pavement after the rain, freshly baked chocolate chip cookies, cinnamon, or cotton candy. What do the different scents remind you of?

What is a scent that reminds you of your childhood? _____

_____

What is a scent that reminds you of a great date? _____

_____

What are scents that remind you of the different seasons?

Spring _____

Summer _____

Fall _____

Winter _____

What three scents can take your muse to an inspired place for the project on which you're working?

1. _____

2. _____

3. _____

There are different ways to tap into your sixth sense: through meditation, dreams, and listening to your gut instincts.

If you have trouble meditating, start by listening to guided meditation CDs. To use your dreams, think about a problem you want answered just as you're falling asleep. You may dream the answer. Be sure to keep a pad and pen by your bed and write your ideas down as soon as you wake up. Sometimes, if you wake up at 4 a.m. and don't write them down, by the time you wake up at 8 a.m. to start your day, you'll have forgotten everything.

Start a project. Pick up an old one or breathe some life into a new one by using one or more of the sensory exercises.

NICK OF TIME

G ene Watson has one hour and fifteen minutes to save his daughter's life. Now that's pressure.

Do you ever feel as if you don't have enough time? Many people I coach see time, or perceived lack of time, as an obstacle. We measure ourselves against other people and what their accomplishments are. The irony is that we all have the same amount of time. Everyone gets the same twenty-four hours in a day. So, if time is stressing you out, the first thing you need to examine is your belief about time. Are you running out of it? Do you believe that if you haven't accomplished certain goals by a certain age that you'll never accomplish them? Is there never enough time in a day? You learned about limiting beliefs in Weeks 23 and 29. What are your limiting beliefs about time?

1. _____

2. _____

Looking at your limiting beliefs, are the consequences true or imagined? Gene Watson was given an ultimatum. He needed to kill someone within a specific time frame or his daughter would be killed. He didn't imagine this. Neither did he create the high stakes, the villains did. To assume that since you're almost thirty-five and you aren't a series regular on a show automatically means you're too old to be one is completely imagined. There's no rule that says people who haven't been series regulars by the age of thirty-five never will be. Why would you want to create unwarranted pressure on yourself? Instead, if you're going to believe something you've imagined, why not imagine a belief that's empowering?

Return to the two beliefs you wrote on the previous page. What empowering beliefs would challenge them? For example, if you wrote, "I never have enough time," the challenging thought could be, "I have plenty of time," or "I have all the time I need to live my dreams."

What are two empowering beliefs about time?

1. _____

2. _____

Once you have two beliefs that empower you, examine how you're spending your time. What percent of your week is spent on/with:

Work _____%		Family _____%
Friends _____%		Necessities* _____%
Exercise _____%		Sleep _____%
Self Care _____%		Other _____%

*driving/commuting, shopping, cooking, etc.

What percentage of your time is spent on work? Is that time being used effectively? If you feel that it's not, review your tools to put together a strategy plan in which you are working smart, not hard. This industry is a marathon, not a sprint. Pace yourself and acknowledge what you're doing to move ahead each day.

After reviewing how you're spending your time, determine if you would like to make changes. If so, start small with fifteen-minute increments. For example, take fifteen minutes from time spent with friends and put them to use by exercising. Or look for opportunities to multi-task. Why not exercise with your friends?

week 44

GROUNDHOG DAY

*I*t's Groundhog Day and Phil Connors, a grouchy weatherman, is forced to cover the story on whether the groundhog will see his shadow. But, the day has a lot to teach Phil when he finds himself living it over and over again.

I had a client who found himself working for "the same boss" on every job. I don't mean that he worked for the same person, I mean that every job he worked on, his bosses treated him with the same disrespect. My client would come to me completely stressed out and second-guessing his capabilities. It became quite clear that he didn't stand up for himself when his bosses crossed specific boundaries.

He expressed a desire to assert himself, but the fear of being fired was too great. His health became compromised from the stress. One day, while working with a new crew, his boss yelled at him in front of everyone. He was so irritable from being sick that he snapped right back at him, pointing out why the mistake was in fact his boss' and not his own. The boss laughed good-naturedly, slapped him on the back, and said, "I like you." He's been happily working with that crew ever since.

243

In *Groundhog Day*, Phil was using his recurring day to glean new information in order to win Rita's heart. He was a quick study of her, but he was not transforming as a person. Therefore, his day continued until he learned his lesson. If you have lessons to learn and you're ignoring them, the same types of people will continually show up in your life to try to teach them to you. An interesting perspective is that you teach others how to treat you. Knowing that, if you don't learn important life lessons, you will continue to teach people to treat you the way others have done. To figure out what life lessons you may need to learn right now, look back on life lessons that you've already learned.

For example, I had a job that I really liked, but I didn't see eye to eye with my boss. He liked the job I did, but he didn't value me enough as an employee to give me a raise. We had different styles of working. I saw him as someone who couldn't make decisions, didn't know how to manage, and wasn't a strong leader, which put his own job in jeopardy. Because he feared for his job, he wouldn't support his staff. This was not necessarily true, but it was how I experienced him, which caused me frustration and stress. Yet, I chose to stay for the security. Finally, I realized a life lesson. My boss was who he was. I couldn't change him or blame him, but I could change my own circumstances by leaving. I could also thank him for being a "teacher" who forced me out of my comfort zone and to take a risk. I learned to value myself and took a chance that paid off!

Who have been the "teachers" throughout your life? What were the valuable lessons they taught you? In other words, who were the unpleasant people in your life—those whose roles in your life you couldn't understand? Now, looking back, can you appreciate the lessons they gave you? Identify your teachers and the lessons:

Teacher: _____

Lesson:_____

Teacher: _____

Lesson:_____

Teacher: _____

Lesson:_____

Looking back on other jobs, I was able to see I was always happy when I worked for bosses who were collaborative and valued their employees. I was always unhappy when I worked for people who didn't appreciate their employees.

Two important factors in the jobs I accept now are collaboration and being valued.

What do you value on the job?

1._____

2._____

3._____

4._____

Sometimes, it's hard to figure out your own life lessons when you're living them. So try out this next exercise and see if you can uncover some patterns.

In the past five years, which negative people (those who pushed your buttons, made you feel bad, insecure, or unworthy) have shown up in your life? (You may want to refer to Week 28)

1. _____

2. _____

3. _____

4. _____

5. _____

6. _____

7. _____

8. _____

Do they share any similar traits?

_____

_____

_____

_____

Do you notice any similarities in the way they've treated you? For example, the common theme can be that they all treat you with disrespect, don't show an appreciation for you, use you, or always need your help.

Common theme: _____

_____

Based on this common theme, what might be the life lesson you need to learn?

Life Lesson: _____

_____

Again, if you don't learn your life lessons, like Phil, you'll be doomed to live the same circumstances over and over again.

1. If you're struggling to come up with your life lesson, share this chapter with people you trust and brainstorm with them. Sometimes, it's easier for those on the outside looking in, to see the

underlying lesson. Be sure that you're open to hearing construc-
tive criticism so your partners feel safe giving you their opinion.

2. Then, take one step this week toward growing from the lesson
you've uncovered.

THAT THING YOU DO! *week* 45

The buzz from a catchy single turns an Erie, Pennsylvania band, The Wonders, into a nationwide sensation. Their manager, Mr. White, adds an extra special touch when he gives drummer Guy Patterson a "trademark look" with a cool pair of shades.

"Buzz" means that people are talking about a person or a project. It's the phenomenon that puts an unknown group like The Wonders into your awareness. The interesting buzz about *That Thing You Do!* was how its unknown actor, Tom Everett Scott, was a young Tom Hanks. Being a Tom Hanks fan since his *Bosom Buddies* days, I saw the movie just to see if indeed the next Tom Hanks had been discovered.

My personal nomination for best buzz goes to Matthew McConaughey's publicity team before the launch of his breakout film, *A Time to Kill*. It was somewhat of a "come to see his butt, stay to see his acting" campaign. It worked. I still see everything he does.

Tom and Matthew were already working and had studio projects to design buzz around. How do you create buzz for yourself if you're an unknown? I'll use getting an agent as an example. Agents get bad reputations because the average person doesn't fully understand the job they do. Most people figure all they need is an agent who can pitch them and submit their reels to casting directors, directors, producers, or studio executives and then they will be hired. But an agent's job is not only about getting you work, it's also about *giving employers what they want*. If you're in production and not on a "studio approved list," it's nearly impossible to get hired. If you're an unknown actor with very few union credits, it's rare that you will book a series regular on a television show. Both of these situations occur, but they're the exception, not the norm. So why would a smart agent take on a large number of unknowns when there's a huge pool of talent who already have established reputations?

This is the part when my clients try to explain the *why* to me, telling me how passionate and talented they are, but again, this is not the exception. Almost every person who has a meeting with an agent pitches himself as passionate and talented. What agents are looking for is someone who is "marketable." With all of the fierce competition, can they sell you? What do you have that no one else has? Or who is willing to hire you?

In Week 32 when you were creating your personal brand, I asked, "How can you make people who hire you perceive you differently from your competitors?" What did you come up with? Do you have a truly unique "new category" or a special skill that an agent can create buzz around? Do you offer a service that no one else does? Bottom line: will you generate enough money to make it worthwhile for an agent to represent you? That's right, agents make a percentage of your earnings, so before they are going to sign you, they have to believe that people are going to hire you.

That's where creating your own buzz meets my strategy for getting an agent:

1. Research the agents who represent your classification and choose at least five agencies to target. If there's any confusion as to which agencies would be a good fit, get advice from people on your Contact List.
2. Once you have your list, research the agency's client list with the goal of finding one client of theirs you know.
3. From your Contact List or mentors, choose two people who have the most industry clout, especially those who are in classifications that hire your classification.
4. Ask your two people from step three and the clients you know from step two to make calls on your behalf to the agents of your choice. You should have three people making calls about you to each of the five agencies.
5. Set up meetings with at least three agencies. This relieves some pressure. If the first meeting doesn't go well, you learn from your mistakes and improve for the next two meetings. If the first meeting goes very well, then the pressure is off for the next two meetings.

The purpose of this strategy is to have three people buzzing about you. If an agent had meetings with ten passionate, talented people how would he choose whom to represent? What if one of the candidates had three people (one of whom the agent already represents and wants to keep happy and two who are in the position to hire) buzzing about how valuable the candidate is?

You can apply this strategy to getting hired for a specific job as well. If you are an editor trying to get hired for a feature, see if any of the hired crew members can make a call on your behalf. Then have your most reputable director and producer contacts make calls to the director who would be hiring you. The goal is to have the agent or the director saying, "I've gotten three calls in one week about this person. Who is she, and why don't I know her?"

If it's a project you want to create buzz around, get creative. I know a writer who wanted to create buzz around a script. He designed three postcards sending each one out to production companies over three weeks as a teaser, tying in the theme of his script. By the third postcard, everyone wanted to know what the script was—and who wrote it.

Research successful independent film campaigns. *The Blair Witch Project* got tons of buzz because people thought it was real.

An actress who had a guest star role on a television series started an e-mail campaign asking all of her friends and family from across the country to write fan letters to the network about her. Her friends and family asked their friends and family and so on and so on.

I produced a television series where all of the series regulars were unknowns, but we cast all of the special guest stars with recognizable talent. Moreover, an actress/producer who had a recurring role in our show was the star of a reality series, so the making of our show was on a network.

Buzz is all about perception. You can create the perception you want by getting creative and asking for help from your contacts.

1. Create a strategy for creating buzz about yourself or your project.

2. List three people who can help you.

    1. _____

    2. _____

    3. _____

3. Make requests for help, break your strategy plan down into manageable tasks, and take your first step this week.

A CHRISTMAS STORY

R alphie Parker has a clear vision of what he wants for Christmas: an official Red Ryder carbine-action 200-shot range model air rifle with a compass in the stock. Ralphie stares at the picture of his dream present and fantasizes about using it. No matter how many times Ralphie is told no, because he'll shoot his eye out, Ralphie continues to dream.

In order to get what you want, you have to know what you want. What can be more specific and clearer than a picture on which to focus? This week, you are going to make a vision board. Having strong, positive, visual symbols can greatly affect your attitude.

To begin, cut out pictures that represent these seven categories:

+ You
+ Your job
+ Finances
+ Personal life
+ Career
+ Life goals
+ Fun

Choose images that you want in your life.

Next choose words and statements for your vision board. Select your words carefully, avoiding any negative statements such as, "I won't be nervous in an interview." Instead say, "I am confident in interviews."

Your subconscious can't distinguish between positive and negative. If I say to you, "Don't think about a big, red dog," the first thing you think of is...

Once you have all your pictures, place them into one of four piles based on how strongly you believe they are obtainable:

1–3   4–6   7–9   10

Note: One means you don't believe you'll get it. Ten means you'll have it without a doubt.

Look at the items that aren't in your "10" pile. What fears are attached to those items that make you believe you can't have them? In your journal, for each picture that you want but don't believe in enough to put in your "10" pile, fill in the following:

Picture: _____

Why I might not get it: _____

_____

_____

Many actresses made their money as waitresses before they got their big breaks. If you were to ask an actress who is now making $10 million a movie and has her own production company if back when she was a waitress she believed with all of her heart that she was going to be such a huge success, she would have said, "Absolutely!" If you then asked her if she was willing to bet her week's tips on it, she might not have been so willing to commit.

We look at the odds of making it, and while we believe we could be one of them, there's a part of us that believes that the chosen ones are the exception to the rule—the miracles.

My question to you is, if there are chosen ones (the miracles), why can't you be one of them? Some of the chosen ones come from Hollywood families, but many others do not. They come from small towns and far away cities. Why can't you be the miracle? Maybe it's because you truly don't believe you can be. If you really believed, you would have every picture of what you want in your "10" pile. Why wouldn't you choose to have faith and believe that you can be the miracle?

The only thing between whatever number you've labeled your pictures and labeling them a "10" is fear. You learned how to visualize what you want in Week 35. To overcome a fear, visualize doing the thing you fear and have it work out exactly as you wish.

For each picture that didn't make it to your "10" pile, see if you can visualize having it the way you want. If you can, then take the leap of faith that you will be the miracle and put the picture into your "10" pile. The power of your conscious decision will let your subconscious mind flow in response to the nature of your thoughts. Now your brain will be in harmony, working consciously and unconsciously to do what it takes to make your visions become your reality.

1. Make your vision board with the images and words from your "10" pile. Using poster board and glue, create a collage that you believe in fully. By doing this, you are setting a very clear intention for yourself and for the universe that this is what you want.

If you are drawn to an image but you don't trust or believe that you can have it, choose it anyway. But note that it is a belief on which you will need to work.

2. Put your vision board in a place where you can see it. Look at it often and feel the feelings of having everything you desire.

week 47
BOWFINGER

D esperate movie producer Bobby Bowfinger fails to get Kit
Ramsey, a major movie star, for his film. As a last resort,
Bobby decides to secretly shoot the film around Kit. Bobby
calls in favors from his friends begging them for help, equipment,
props, and time worked for free. Because his friends believe in
Bowfinger, his project, and its star, Kit Ramsey, the group takes
outrageous risks to get *Chubby Rain* made.

Making choices and taking career risks means taking respon-
sibility for your career. I receive numerous calls a week from clients
who have career decisions to make and want me to tell them what
to choose. They could be choosing between two job offers on projects that shoot simultaneously. One is a small production with a
client who keeps them busy and basically pays the bills. The other is
with a big production and a new crew. If they take the big production, it could lead to bigger, better work, but they risk losing their
small client.

Another scenario is being offered a job for no pay. The script is
good, but there's no recognizable talent.

There are also opportunities to work on big projects with a

259

disreputable person. Basically, they'd be stuck working for a big jerk.

They ask me for the decision because if I give them an answer, (which I don't) and they don't like the outcome, they can blame me.

The bottom line is, placing blame doesn't change anything. Decision making can be hard because it involves some dissatisfaction or mental struggle. You have to learn how to make a decision for yourself and to accept the consequences, whatever the outcome may be.

Unfortunately, there is no crystal ball that can predict the outcomes of our choices. That's why so many decisions are considered risks. But you can take steps to make the most educated decisions for you and your family. The goal in decision making is to choose the circumstances in which the possibilities for a positive outcome outweigh the possible losses.

Here are some steps for making good decisions:

1. Identify the struggle of your decision. What problem needs to be solved and why?
2. What are all of the factors involved in your choices?
3. On what values are you judging the different alternatives? Looking at the first example on the previous page, the client had to choose between two job opportunities. He valued loyalty and financial stability in the first possibility, and growth, establishing new relationships, and new opportunity in the second.

4. Brainstorm the possible outcomes of your choices. Determine if there are any possibilities that you haven't considered by brainstorming with other people.

5. Evaluate your choices by what you have to gain and what you have to lose. These should include both physical gains/losses and the emotional gains/losses based on your values from step three.

6. Make your decision based on steps one through five.

7. Evaluate the outcome of your decision and determine any lessons that you've learned.

It's important to practice the decision-making process on simple everyday choices because many times you're forced into a situation in which you quickly have to make your decision.

If you don't have time to go through the steps on the previous page, trust your gut. What was the first thought that popped into your head when you were given your choice? That little voice that yelled out something to you, what did it say?

Sometimes, your gut is in line with your protective habits and will immediately start yelling out things to keep you safe. It's moments like these when you have to decide if you want to take a risk.

To get your gut in line with the decision making process, you must develop a clear motivation for your career. Reread the example at the beginning of this chapter. If the client's motivation is to take his career to the next level, and he knows in his heart and soul that he has to take certain risks to achieve this, his intuitive voice that first speaks up will tell him, "Go for the big production, take the risk." If his motivation in his career is financial stability, then his intuitive voice will probably shout, "Sticking with what you know will keep bringing in the dough."

We are constantly being influenced by short-term satisfaction. In Week 1, you considered where you want to be in twenty years. The choices you make today will influence where you are in the future. When weighing the outcomes from step four, imagine you're retired and looking back on the decisions you've made. How does the retirement of your dreams reflect the choices you've made? How have they influenced your career?

Write a clear motivational statement for your career.

_____

_____

_____

_____

HITCH

Alex Hitchens is a "date doctor" who personally advises his clients on how to date the woman of their dreams. Through extensive research and one-on-one training, Alex connects seemingly unlikely couples, including awkward Albert, who's trying to win the heart of the rich and powerful Allegra Cole.

It is so rewarding to be a "connector" like Hitch, creating the opportunities to bring people together who otherwise wouldn't meet. You've spent a lot of time working on meeting new people and re-establishing relationships. This week's focus will be on connecting the people you know.

Here are just a few of the many reasons to undertake this task:

+ You are helping your friends meet people who can potentially help/hire them.
+ Through connecting others you could become connected to the people they know.
+ You create a community of like-minded people.

I had a client who wanted to meet new people. He lived in an exclusive area just outside of Los Angeles that had a pretty big entertainment industry community. He decided to tap into that community by creating a networking opportunity for the people who lived there. That they would be meeting new people without having to travel into the city was the draw.

He started by inviting about ten people he knew in different classifications, (actors, writers, directors, DPs, composers, producers) to a local restaurant. He said he wanted to introduce them to each other. It was such a successful evening that he suggested they do it again the next month with each person inviting an entertainment industry guest. At the following gathering the number of people doubled in size, and my client met a whole new group of people.

There are many great ideas for becoming a connector. If you're called for work that you are unable to take, connect the employer with one of your contacts. Too many people feel competitive in this industry. That comes from the fear that there's not enough work to go around. My theory is, wouldn't you rather your contact get the job than a complete stranger? If your contact accepts it, then perhaps he will pass your name along when the shoe is on the other foot. You can trust your contact more than a stranger. Also, if your contact is working, you can visit him on set, which can put you in the right place at the right time.

You can connect people for work outside of your classification. If you're a production designer who knows a handful of directors, why not introduce them to other people you know: other heads of departments (DPs, editors, costumers, etc), actors, and producers? Who knows, you may all wind up working together on the director's next project!

Why not start a filmmaking group or a script workshop group? In Los Angeles and beyond, proactive people who wanted to create their own opportunities have started filmmaking groups where they bring together people of all classifications and make short films and commercials. Check out some of these proactive people at www.group101.com, www.group101spots.com, www.instantfilms.com, and www.48hourfilm.com. There are many others out there, but I've attended screenings from these particular groups and they are great models for you. Another option is a script workshop group where writers bring their scripts and actors read the material. It's a great way for actors to be seen, writers to get feedback, and producers and directors to find material.

You can throw a party at your home or like my client, pick a local spot and have people meet there. It can be loose, or you can create a theme that has people interacting with each other.

If you already have outside interests you share with some of your contacts like sports, biking, kids, or dogs, why not make it a group event with everyone bringing likeminded contacts? There are many industry leagues. Why not start your own?

1. Who are the contacts you can connect right now?

_____ & _____

_____ & _____

_____ & _____

_____ & _____

_____ & _____

2. Choose an option for connecting at least two of your contacts this week.

FORREST GUMP

*T*he interesting travels of Forrest Gump, a man with a low IQ, cause him to be present during many significant historical events. Through heartache and loss, Forrest finds success in every step along the way. After all, his momma taught him, "Life was like a box of chocolates. You never know what you're gonna get."

Forrest had a positive outlook on life because he was always looking for the good. Know what you want, create a clear picture of how it will happen, and be sure that you're able to recognize it once you've accomplished it. This may be more challenging than you think. The reason for this is simple and I will explain it to you after you answer the following question:

When will you know you've "made it?" _____

_____

_____

_____

_____

What seems like "making it" to you today, will change as your career advances. We have become very familiar with overnight sensations: people who get catapulted to superstardom from obscurity. This is the exception to the rule. Most people go from one small success to the next small success to the next one. When this happens, you lose sight of what you first considered "making it" because you're always focused on what comes next.

Let's use an actor whose idea of "making it" is to be cast in a good part on a scripted television show. The actor gets a few co-stars. His friends congratulate him, but he says, "It's no big deal, just a co-star." Then he gets a few guest stars. His friends congratulate him, but he says, "It's no big deal, just a guest star." Then he gets a recurring role on a television show. His friends congratulate him, but he says, "It's no big deal, I'm not a series regular." Then he gets a series regular on a pilot. His friends congratulate him, but he says, "Don't get excited, it hasn't been picked up yet." Then his pilot gets picked up. His friends congratulate him, but he says, "Don't get excited, we don't know how long it will last." Then it lasts, becoming a big success and his friends congratulate him, but he says, "Whatever, it's just TV. What I really want is a movie."

According to his vision of what "making it" was, being cast in a good part on a scripted television show was it. Yet, he never celebrated the little successes of "making it." By the time he was a series regular, he was too busy concerning himself with what he wanted next (a feature film role). He had, in fact, "made it."

This is an extremely stressful way to go through life. It is so important to celebrate all successes, big and small. To celebrate them, you first have to get into the habit of acknowledging them. Have you ever noticed that when you ask a four-year-old what she did that day she will give you a list that sounds something like, "I played ball and pet my dog. I ate a sandwich for lunch and smelled a flower on our bush..." all with the tonality of such excitement and pride that you would think she'd won an Academy Award. When you're young, everything seems possible, wonderful, exciting, and new. Everything is an accomplishment.

Then, as you grow up, people start giving you commentary and, worse, criticism on what you consider an accomplishment until finally all you care about is what comes next.

This week, you're going to get back in touch with your inner four-year-old, and start getting excited about every step you take along the way of your career journey. Now, if you're a pessimist you might be thinking, "But if I don't celebrate my accomplishments, I can't be disappointed." That may be true, but it's not a very satisfying way to go through life!

List your five biggest career successes from the past eleven months:

1._____

2._____

3._____

4._____

5._____

List five small successes you've experienced over the last eleven months:

1._____

2._____

3._____

4._____

5._____

Get into the habit of acknowledging yourself for three successes everyday, even if they're as simple as, "I took a walk and took some time to smell the roses."

In your journal, write three successes for each day this week. I recommend that you continue this practice after the week is through—but that is up to you.

week 50
JERRY MAGUIRE

"Twenty-four hours ago, man I was hot! Now... I'm a cautionary tale. You see this jacket I'm wearing? You like it? I don't really need it, because I'm cloaked in failure! I lost the number one draft pick the night before the draft...Why? Let's recap. Because a hockey player's son made me feel like a superficial jerk, I ate two slices of bad pizza, went to bed, grew a conscience..."

What Jerry Maguire was referring to when he said, "Grew a conscience," was the mission statement he had written and distributed to his entire company—a company of sports agents who were not exactly in the business of concerning themselves with the well-being of others. Jerry was fired, cast out on his own with only his assistant and a single client, determined to build his own company with a conscience.

How could a mission statement lead to the swift termination of a hugely successful member of the sports agency's team?

A mission statement is a simple and clear declaration of who you are, what you're committed to, and what you exist to do. Jerry's mission changed from that of his company. They perceived his new

271

mission as a threat to the way they worked, so he was fired.

Why is having a mission statement so important that I'm dedicating an entire chapter to it so close to the end of this book?

In Week 47, your "And... Action" assignment was to write out a clear motivation statement for your career. The motivation statement is a tool to help you make important choices. The mission statement is a tool to guide both your career and life.

I've chosen the end of this book to introduce this tool because you've had eleven months for learning new business tools, creating better habits, assimilating empowering beliefs, and gaining control over your emotions. After this experience, you have grown and changed. It is time to declare who you are, what you're committed to, and maybe even why you're here.

A mission statement can create clarity, help you make decisions according to your values, inspire and motivate you, and explain your goals to others.

There is no right or wrong way to write a mission statement. If I had to give you directions, I'd say make it your own and have it come from your heart. Here is a portion of my mission statement:

I will strive to take care of myself as well as I take care of others and empower others to take care of themselves.

I will always make time for my family and make them feel cherished.

I will make my parents proud every day.

I will say "I love you" more.

I will hold strong to my values and integrity.

I will ask for help and be open to receiving it.

I will always have big dogs.

I will have a water theme in my home and spend
more time in nature.

I will travel and experience other cultures
as well as take pampering vacations.

I will always make time for creative outlets and things I enjoy.

I will be charitable both by donation
and personal involvement.

I will always be giving others the opportunity to succeed.

I will take my position as a role model seriously, carefully
making choices that reflect my values and portray positive images.

I will make the kind of movies that will touch people's lives so
that for two hours they can feel swept away from reality and
affected by my story or character.

I will work to educate, to empower,
and to motivate young people.

I will find and live "balance."

I will strive to live in a less violent world.

I will always trust that whatever I'm doing is what I should be doing and that everything happens for a reason.

I will always work to be the best person I can be.

To create your own mission statement start by filling out the simple "I will" form.

MISSION STATEMENT dated: _____/_____/_____

I will _____

_____

I will _____

_____

I will _____

_____

I will _____

_____

I will _____

_____

I will _____

_____

Continue in your journal with as many "I will" statements as you can. The format and presentation are up to you. You can keep it in the "I will" format, put it into a summary paragraph, or design your own presentation. Personalize it with your own visual touches.

1. Incorporate your mission statement into your life: be the person you want to be, do the things you want to do, etc.

2. Put the statement where you can see it: in your office, on your nightstand, in your car, in your bathroom. Be energized by it!

OCEAN'S ELEVEN

With his latest heist planned, recently paroled Danny Ocean is thinking big, as in robbing Las Vegas casinos, big. To pull off such an elaborate plan, Danny needs help. He goes around the country to assemble a team of experts such as his right-hand man, a retired thief, a pickpocket, an explosives expert, two front men, a bitter casino mogul, a professional card dealer, a surveillance man, and a Chinese acrobat.

In this second-to-last chapter, I want to address the importance of assembling your success team. They will help you maintain the momentum you've created this year by doing this work. A success team is a group of like-minded individuals who want support, motivation, accountability, growth, commitment, and success in their careers. You can find people in the same classification as you, or you can mix it up. A success team is created for the following reasons: to push you beyond what you normally do, to help you achieve specific and challenging goals, and to brainstorm solutions.

You learned in Week 24 that many people in the entertainment industry feel they have to do it alone. Well, you learned that's not true. And what's even more accountable than a partnership is being a part of a success team.

Here's how it works:

1. Review your Contact List and find nine other people who are interested in being a part of a success team.
2. Decide if you want to meet once a week or once a month. I don't recommend going longer than a month.
3. Choose someone to be the group leader. The leader can rotate with each meeting or remain the same.
4. Have the leader choose a topic for the group to discuss in the meeting. The leader can do this on her own or ask the team for suggestions. You can also use this book as a guide. If you meet once a week, you can use the specified topic. If you meet once a month, you can start with the first week and have everyone check in through e-mail once a week regarding the next three chapters.
5. After addressing the topic, the group leader will guide the group in a discussion of any obstacles that need brainstorming.
6. Have all group members pair up into accountability partners. Commit to calling your partner a few times a week to check in. During these calls, you will tell him what you've done, what you need to do before your next call, and what you're stuck on. Your partner will do the same. These need not be long phone calls.
7. Have all group members share e-mail addresses so the team leader can e-mail a master list to everyone. In this way, group

members can share their progress with the team a few days
per week. Here's a template for the group e-mail:

Partner's name:
Goal for week/month:
Action plan for week/month:
What I will accomplish today:
Requests for the team:

Then you can add fun ones like:

Good deed for the day:
Smartest business move of the day:
Other ideas or words of wisdom:

Be open to the following possibilities: everyone on your team can
help you in some way, everyone you need to know can be accessed
through this team, and every obstacle you encounter can be overcome with the power of teamwork.

The team leader can create guidelines for the group in the
vein of:

I promise to work ethically and with integrity.
I promise to consider everyone's goal in this group to be as
    important as my own. (After all, if one person on your
    team falls behind, the dynamic of the whole team can be

thrown off).

I promise to celebrate other team members' successes and to help those who get off track.

I promise to acknowledge my own success and to ask for help when I need it.

Should team members need to leave the group for work or personal reasons, bring in someone to replace them. These are loose parameters to use as a guide for creating a team that works for you.

Whether or not you achieve your goal in the week's/month's time, by giving 100 percent to being a team player, you will achieve results that will continue to pay off for the rest of your career.

Assemble your success team.

week 52
ROCKY

Rocky Balboa's whole life is a million-to-one shot. As a small-time boxer who makes his living working in a meat factory and collecting debts for a loan shark, Rocky never stops believing in his dream of being a heavyweight champion. Rocky never, ever gives up!

Congratulations! You made it to Week 52! You are already more committed and more informed than the majority of the people trying to break into this industry. Clearly you, like Rocky, have a determined mindset for success!

To maintain and master a tenacious mindset, do the following:

1. Continue to take action
2. Evaluate whether your actions are working
3. If they aren't working try something new
4. Repeat one through three

Why you can persevere and succeed:

- You now have a clear understanding of the rollercoaster ride that is our industry. You know you can find supplemental or parallel income to maintain stability.
- You have clear goals and a business plan. You know what you want in your future.
- You have tools to market yourself.
- You have solid contacts and mentors. You know how to seek out new people and create relationships with them.
- You have tools and templates to organize yourself.
- You have mindsets to keep you patient, motivated, inspired, and emotionally sound.
- You know that successful people feel fear but act in spite of it.
- You are empowered to create your own opportunities and projects.
- You know how to attract what you want and need, to look for serendipities, and to be grateful as you grow.
- You understand the importance of maintaining balance in all areas of your life.
- You give back to others, and that makes you feel good.
- You know how to create partnerships and a success team.

With all you have learned and achieved in the last year, trust that you have planted many seeds. Enjoy watching them sprout into beautiful blooms. This will happen in due time and in unexpected places and ways.

As long as you love what you do, never, ever give up!

1. Give yourself a reward! You've earned it!

2. Give yourself the gifts of maintaining your good work habits and momentum.

My final words to you are: Be conscious of who you're being in the industry. No matter how talented you are or how big of a star you may be, people remember you if you are a good and kind person—but they really remember you (in negative ways) if you are obnoxious and troublesome.

Be kind and respectful to everyone you meet and don't make outrageous demands because today's PA is tomorrow's Studio Head, and people have great memories.

If questions come up while working on this book, please e-mail me at *jessica@thegreenlightcoach.com* or visit my Web site at *www.thegreenlightcoach.com*.

Good luck with everything you do. I sincerely wish you all the success that you dream about!

ABOUT THE AUTHOR

J essica Sitomer has worked in the entertainment industry for eighteen years as a writer, an independent producer, a development associate, a director, and an actress. For twelve of those years she was a career coach for Entertainment Industry Professionals. Within that period she served for seven years as the in-house career coach for the International Cinematographers Guild.

In January 2008, Ms. Sitomer launched her own business, The Greenlight Coach. People involved in all areas of the industry attend her ongoing Group Intensive Program. She speaks professionally to the entertainment industry and has designed thirty-five seminars. Her twelve-month Career Growth Series includes sessions on business tools, successful interviewing, getting meetings, overcoming fear, finding stability in an unstable industry, and creating career breakthroughs. Another component of her business is one-on-one career development coaching. She is a certified results coach and a certified practitioner of creation technologies.

Following the production of two television pilots, Ms. Sitomer is currently in pre-production on a feature film that she wrote and is co-directing. She continues to write, act, and produce. She also publishes coaching articles. *AND... ACTION!* is Jessica Sitomer's first book.

LaVergne, TN USA
01 September 2009
156618LV00002B/148/P